The Internet for Schools

A practical step-by-step guide for teachers,
student teachers, parents and governors

Internet Handbooks

Books & Publishing on the Internet
Building a Business in Cyberspace
Chat on the Internet
Email for Beginners
Find it on the Internet
Finding a Job on the Internet
Free Stuff on the Net
Gardens & Gardening on the Internet
History on the Internet
Homes & Property on the Internet
Internet for Schools
Internet for Students
Internet for Writers
Kids' Stuff on the Internet
Law & Lawyers on the Internet
Medicine & Health on the Internet
Personal Finance on the Internet
School Web Site
Shops & Shopping on the Internet
Travel & Holidays on the Internet
Wildlife & Conservation on the Internet

Other titles in preparation

The Internet for Schools

A practical step-by-step guide for teachers, student teachers, parents and governors

Barry Thomas & Richard Williams

Internet Handbooks

Contents

List of illustrations

· ·

Preface

The aim of this volume is to provide a gentle introduction to the internet for teachers and others involved in education. It is not meant for students; there is a companion volume designed to meet the needs of young people: *The Internet for Students* by David Holland. The focal point is on the UK educational system and the level is clear: it is for beginners.

Each chapter is self-contained, so the book does not have to be read in serial order. After reading the initial chapter you can dip in and out where you like. Each chapter contains questions and answers and many case studies based on real-life experiences.

With the aid of more than 90 illustrations we have tried to explain and present much of the content in visual as well as textual terms.

This is a practical book but if you are a complete beginner to, say, email, you would be advised to supplement this volume with the sister publication on using electronic mail where there will obviously be a lot more detail.

At the end of the book we have listed web sites that are referred to in each chapter. We have tried to avoid the usual massive lists seen in so many other books on the internet. We have been rather selective because we realise that sites are apt to disappear or move with frequency.

The government has decided that all teachers should reach a good level of IT skills by the year 2002. We hope that this book will make a contribution to this important initiative.

A lynchpin of government policy is the establishment of the National Grid for Learning. In late 1998 this was still in its development stage, but with pledged lottery money it promises to become a significant engine for educational change in the future – and it is to take place through the medium of the internet. It is the hope of the authors that practising (and knowledgeable) teachers will play an active part in forming and shaping the Grid.

Barry Thomas would like to thank Graham Lawlor of Lime Avenue Education for all his help and support during the writing of this book; also all his colleagues at Landau Forte College where there is such enthusiasm for the use of IT. Special thanks go to colleagues Chris Stammers and Marc Charles for help and advice over the past year.

Preface ···

Dedications

Barry Thomas would like to dedicate this volume to the teachers of:

> Henry Thornton School, Clapham, London
> Landau Forte College, Derby
> Rushey Mead School, Leicester.

Staff at all these schools have made a contribution to this book in some important way.

Richard Williams would like to dedicate this volume to Juliette.

Barry Thomas and Richard Williams

1 What is the internet and why use it?

In this chapter you will be introduced to the following topics:

▶ *the early history of the internet*
▶ *the main uses of the internet*
▶ *the educational uses of the internet*
▶ *where you need to take care on the internet.*

Development and history (brief!)

The internet is a worldwide network consisting of thousands of smaller networks scattered around the globe. The internet is not in one place, or 'owned' by anyone. The 'internet' has rapidly evolved into a very broad concept, and could be likened to a term like 'the printed word' – the term we use to encompass all books and magazines.

Its origins go back to the late 1960s when the US government set up an experimental project known as ARPANET (Advanced Research Project Agency) which later became the Defence Advanced Research Project Agency (DARPANET). The aim was to enable computer networks across the USA to continue to communicate with each other if some of the networks were destroyed by Russian attack.

At first only four computers were linked together by a computer protocol system called the Internet Protocol (IP).

The universities were allowed to link to DARPANET to enable academic research papers to flow between them. In 1991 the US government removed its ban on the commercial use of the internet.

Today the internet is a vast system of inter-communicating networks financed by business, governments and educational bodies. It now links 150 countries and is rapidly growing from day to day. Thousands of UK schools are now linked to the internet at some level.

The internet is not just the web!

It is a mistake to believe that the internet is synonymous with the world wide web. As you will see below the web is only one reason why you should connect your computer to the internet.

What does the internet consist of?

Basically there are five main components of the internet:

1. electronic mail (or 'email' for short)
2. usenet
3. the world wide web (the 'web')

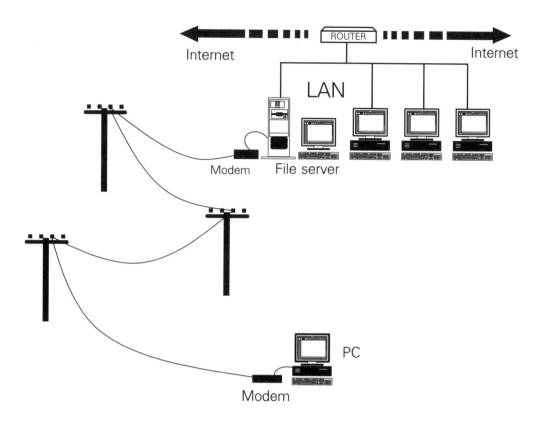

Fig. 1. Connecting a PC to
the internet.

4. telnet

5. file transfer protocol (or FTP).

Electronic mail

Email is a means of almost instantly sending letters and other files
including multi-media ones from one machine to another anywhere in
the world. There are now some 100 million emails a day being sent
world wide.

Usenet

Usenet is a worldwide and ever-expanding collection or network of
interest groups or newsgroups. They allow people with all kinds of
similar interests to share ideas.

World wide web

The web provides an almost standard means of transferring information in hypermedia form. These documents are not machine specific,
so they can be viewed on different types of computer.

Telnet

Telnetting allows you to connect to another computer on a distant
network.

File transfer protocol

FTP is a very useful means of sending files of any type (such as programs, documents and graphics) from one computer to another.

Questions and answers

What is a network?
A network consists of a number of computers connected together by cable, radio satellite, and infrared or microwave links.

What is a protocol?
A protocol is a set of rules that allows different computer systems to communicate with one another.

What do we mean by multimedia?
Multimedia files can consist of

▷ photographs
▷ video-clips
▷ sound.

What is a web browser?
A web browser is a program that allows you to view pages on the world wide web and make use of **hypertext links**. Hypertext links allow you to jump between pages on one site, and jump to pages on another site.

What equipment do I need?

All types of computer can be connected to the internet – with varying degrees of ease! These include:

▷ PCs (personal computers) running Windows 3.1x, Windows 95, or Windows 98
▷ Apple Macintoshes
▷ Acorn RISCOS machines
▷ UNIX workstations
▷ supercomputers, minicomputers and mainframes.

Most new computers bought by the general public, schools and businesses are PCs, so the illustrations in this book will refer to this type of computer. However, the information here is still appropriate to Apple and Acorn users.

In addition to your computer you need:

▷ a modem or ISDN adapter (if using an ISDN connection)
▷ the appropriate software
▷ the services of an internet provider.

Educational uses of the internet ....

Chapter 2 will give you the information you need to get yourself connected.

What are the educational uses of the internet?

The three main uses of the internet for schools are:

1. communicating information

2. obtaining resources and

3. publishing educational materials.

Communicating information

Let's look at these elements in turn and match them with the resources that comprise the internet.

Electronic mail

This allows students to communicate with each other and with their teachers at home or across the globe. They can share information and documents, and be involved in all kinds of curriculum projects.

Usenet

Usenet is a **bulletin board system** (BBS). Writers 'post' items to discussion areas on the internet that can be read with the aid of special 'news reading' software. There are over 28,000 of these discussion groups. This area of the internet contains much dross but also many useful items. The 'uk.education' groups and the US-based 'K12' groups are useful places to visit in order to keep in touch with current developments on the web. However, parts of usenet at present are prone to **spamming** (being flooded with junk messages).

Fig. 2. Starting an email project.

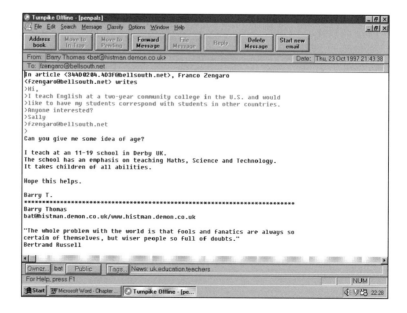

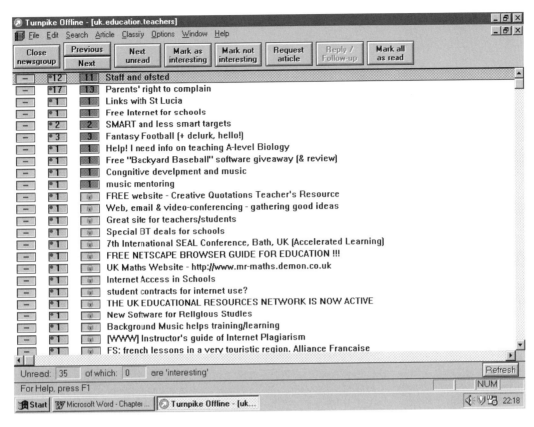

Mailing lists

These are special interest discussion groups that work in a slightly different way to usenet. They have the advantage that many of them are **moderated**. This means to some extent they are censored. These lists are free to join and are operated through the means of email. The level of discussion is usually high.

Fig. 3. A usenet page from the main educational newsgroup for UK teachers.

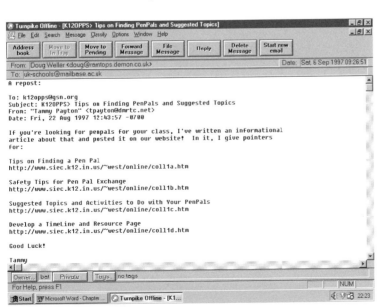

Fig. 4. An email from the uk-schools list on finding key pals (pen friends in old language!).

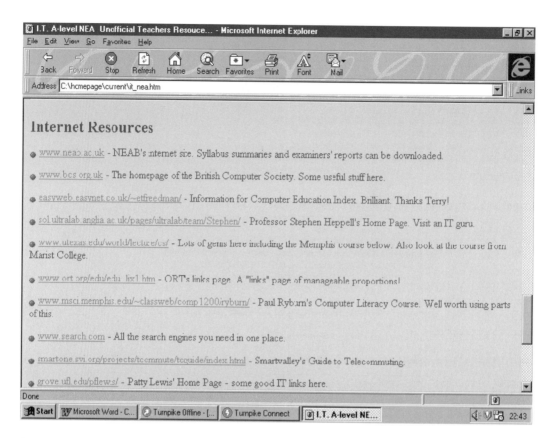

Fig. 5. A web page from the author's site, using Microsoft's Internet Explorer web browser.

Most of the UK mailing lists can be found at Newcastle University's mailbase computer. More details of this can be found in Chapter 5.

Video-conferencing

Video-conferencing is not part of the internet and is still in its early stages when used over this medium. However, it will undoubtedly become important over the next few years. Its use lies in allowing students to communicate with others, especially with those abroad.

This would be particularly beneficial, for example, to modern language teaching. Students and staff can share programs and data between institutions. Even the teachers could be shared amongst several schools. **Whiteboarding** is now often used alongside video-conferencing. This allows images on a whiteboard in one class to be seen in another. These boards can also be used like large screen monitors.

Obtaining resources

The world wide web

The web contains a vast and ever-increasing mass of information for students, teachers and parents. However, much of this is unstructured and of varying quality. Much care is needed when using the web because it can be a massive time-waster and it does harbour unsuitable materials. However, there are many gems to be found, and much material on the web is unavailable elsewhere.

File transfer protocol

FTP allows files – including software – to be **downloaded** to your computer (the 'local' computer) from another computer (the 'remote' computer). These files could include, for example:

▷ worksheets
▷ clip art
▷ music
▷ digitised images.

In the same way, you can also **upload** files from your computer to a computer site somewhere else. You can use special software to access a site through FTP. However, most web browsers can handle FTP sessions. These include the two most popular browsers, Microsoft internet Explorer and Netscape Navigator. These tend to be slightly slower and less sophisticated than the specialised software but are perfectly serviceable.

Publishing material

Many schools and individuals are now running their own web sites just like thousands of businesses. Publishing web pages is not difficult these days. There are several user-friendly programs to help you. We will discuss the construction of web pages in later chapters (see Chapters 8 and 9).

Issues involving the use of the internet

We have said above that the internet has many uses in education. However, there are some basic issues to be aware of:

▷ There is a vast mass of content (on the web and usenet), much of it not indexed or found in indexes. Over a million new web pages a week are being added.

▷ All search programs – such as Yahoo!, AltaVista or Infoseek – are variable in their cover of material on the internet. Get to know how the different search programs and directories work (see Chapter 6).

▷ There is much unsuitable material on the internet (on the web and usenet) which is accessible to students unless you use a **filtered service**. Companies such as Research Machines and BT Campus World provide such a filtering service. The important issue of filtering will be dealt with in Chapter 7.

▷ Searching the internet can be one of the greatest time-wasting exercises of all time! This fact means that students (and all users) need to be taught high-level information-handling skills. Think about your task before rushing on to the internet to find something. Using pencil and paper to define your areas of study would be a good way to start.

Questions and answers ....

▷ UK use of the internet can work out expensive, particularly since we have to pay phone charges on top of payments to a company that provides our internet link. This contrasts with the USA where many users have long enjoyed free local phone calls.

▷ Don't believe everything you find on the internet. Much of it does not have the credibility of a good encyclopaedia (book or multimedia CD-ROM).

Questions and answers

What is meant by hypermedia?
These are links on a web page to text, graphics and sound etc.

What is spamming?
Yes, there is a Monty Python connection! Spamming is net jargon for sending the same message to a large number of mailboxes or newsgroups. The material is frequently offensive and always unwelcome. But there are ways of eliminating it with anti-spamming software.

Will I ever need to telnet?
Probably not. Some internet providers require you to use a telnet program to change your access password.

What is an internet address?
An IP is something needed by every computer on the internet. The address is the computer's IP or internet protocol. The IP address consists of 4 sets of numbers separated by dots such as 158.152.1.43.

Summary

In this chapter we have briefly looked at the history of the internet, its main uses especially educational ones and some issues to bear in mind when accessing it. In the next chapter will investigate how to connect to the internet, who to communicate with, and what basic hardware you will need.

2 Getting connected is not difficult

In this chapter you will be introduced to the following topics:

▶ *what you need in order to get connected to the internet with a dial-up connection*
▶ *what the difference is between an internet service provider and an on-line service provider*
▶ *the software and hardware you need*
▶ *the relative costs and pros and cons of dial-up, ISDN and cable connections.*

. . . .

Dial-up connection

Over the next few years, **dial-up connections** will continue to be the way teachers at home, parents and small schools will usually access the internet. By a dial-up connection we mean that you access the internet with your PC using a modem (or ISDN adapter) which is connected to your telephone line.

Large secondary schools might consider a permanent connection for their networks in the form of a leased line.

With a dial-up link, you are in reality 'renting' a connection from a company that has direct internet connections and acts as a gateway for you. You pay a monthly or perhaps a yearly fee and the internet provider enables you to attach to its computers. You are able to access the internet and are given an email account (or perhaps several).

As you are more than likely to be using a PC it is advisable to have one with Windows 95 or Windows 98 installed. This is easier to configure than earlier versions of Windows such as Windows 3.1 which are not very internet friendly. Moreover there is a wealth of expertise available on the internet for users of Windows 95. So why re-invent the wheel?

Service providers

There are two main types of service provider that will give you access to the internet. They are:

▷ **Internet service providers**, or ISPs for short. They include Demon, BT, Pipex Dial, Virgin and Research Machines.

▷ **Online service providers,** or OSPs for short. They include AOL (America Online), the Microsoft Network (MSN), and LineOne (owned by BT and News International).

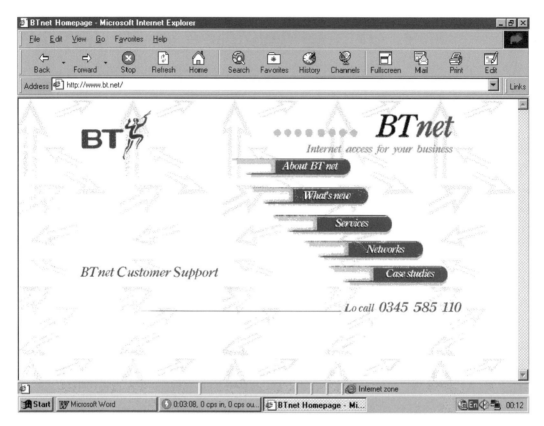

Fig. 6. BTnet is now a major UK internet service provider.

Internet service providers

These companies provide a direct internet connection and the necessary software to do this. The large companies such as Demon, BT and Pipex Dial have the ability to provide a massive number of connections to the internet. They can support thousands of simultaneous users. They can afford large and very fast machines to provide rapid email delivery and vast numbers of usenet discussion groups. Smaller companies, whose adverts also pepper computer magazines, usually lease their capacity from larger ones. They often do not offer the same facilities, reliability and speed.

What to look for

Any company worth considering as your service provider should offer the following:

▷ Support by email or telephone – *available 24 hours per day.*

▷ Local telephone access number – *allowing cheap local phone calls.*

▷ Web page space – *5 Mb minimum (sufficient for an individual or small school).*

▷ Suitable software for accessing the net – *preferably an integrated suite of programs.*

▷ Quality documentation – *a handbook or detailed help files.*

> **Tip!** Some companies offer special deals to schools and teachers. Research Machines offer a special home rate for teachers outside normal school hours. AOL, MSN and Enterprise offer free accounts for schools. You will find their web addresses on pages 142–3.

Online service providers

The alternative to using an ISP is to join an online service provider such as AOL. The software for this type of provider is readily available. Most glossy computer magazines have them on special offer in the form of CDs, usually with 30 days' free trial.

As a member of such a service you can access the internet and a mass of information specially developed by the service. The OSP provides sections about sport, games, travel etc that is not available *in that format* to the general internet user.

Costs of online service providers

You need to be aware that browsing through these areas can be addictive and time-wasting – exactly like the internet itself. The providers seek to tempt you with their own menus of news, sport, education, entertainment, members' areas and similar attractions.

Fig. 7. AOL (America Online) is an OSP with lots of offers to encourage you to join!

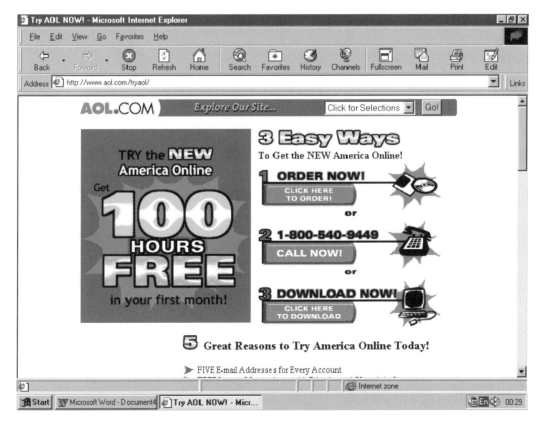

Free trial offers

Moreover, most OSPs charge for access to their services above a basic minimum time allowance.

When the internet was in its infancy (only a few years ago!) using an OSP was very appealing, and AOL, for example, became very popular for that reason. Access to the internet was not easy outside universities, and the world wide web itself was new and undeveloped. However, today most of the information that OSPs offer is freely available elsewhere to internet users through the aid of powerful search programs and vast internet directories.

Taking out a free trial

If you are connecting from home, it is a good idea to dip your toes into the water via a free trial with one of these companies. However, most require a credit card account to be quoted in order to join the free trial.

If you decide not to continue with the OSP don't forget to cancel the account at the end of the trial. To be on the safe side I would suggest that you cover all aspects by phoning, emailing and writing to the company concerned!

Here is a summary of the main differences between an ISP and an OSP:

ISP	OSP
Direct internet access. You can use any internet software you wish.	Internet access within online service. You may not be able to easily use non-OSP software such as newsreaders.
Usually you pay a flat monthly or yearly fee.	Usually you pay a fee for a set number of hours. Additional hours attract extra charges.
Usually a set up charge is made.	No set up charges.
Relatively little or no extra content	Online databases, chat rooms and some special educational material such as the Anglia material on AOL and the projects on BT's Campus World.
100% local telephone charges	100% local telephone charges should be available.

Software

Whatever company you subscribe to, you will be supplied with software to make your internet connection. This software will consist

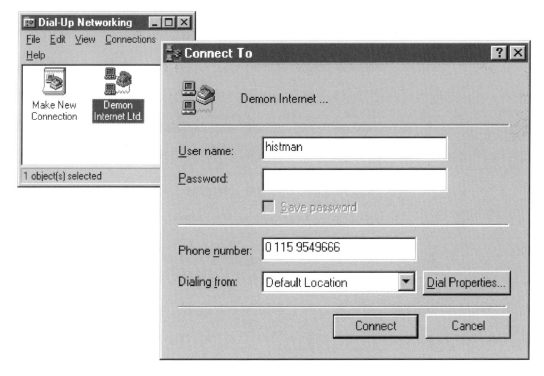

of a TCP/IP package (commonly known as a **stack**) and a **dialling program**.

If you have Windows 95 or Windows 98 you have this software already installed, though how to use it may not be obvious. Most internet providers will send you instructions on how to configure these elements or provide you with the components pre-configured. Some companies provide you (often at a price) with a completely integrated suite of programs which allows you to do everything you need to do on the internet (browse, ftp, email and read news etc). Demon, for example, will sell you its Turnpike suite. Many of the larger companies provide a CD-ROM with all the necessary fixtures to connect quickly.

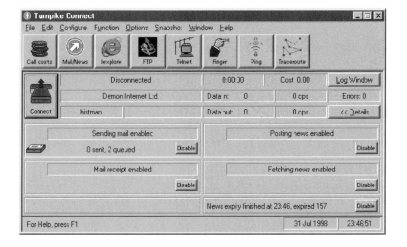

Modems

The hardware you need

Modems

You need a **modem** to connect your computer via your telephone line to the remote computer belonging to your ISP or OSP. These can be internal or external to your machine; generally speaking external modems are easier to set up for beginners.

There are many brands of modem but in the end all they do is transmit and receive data. They should not cost more than about £100. You should aim to buy the fastest you can buy in order to save money on your telephone bills but you must make sure that your internet provider supports the speed you have chosen.

Modem speeds
Modems are usually referred to by the speed at which they transmit data. The speed is measured in kilobits per second or Kbps. You should aim for a 56Kbps modem.

The 56Kbps modem
Until recently there has been a problem, however, in that there were two formats for the 56Kbps standard. These were (or are):

X2	produced by 3COM (US Robotics)
K56flex	produced by Hayes and Motorola, amongst others.

Thankfully, in late 1998 a new standard, V90, was ratified for 56Kbps modems. It should be possible to upgrade these machines (X2 and K56flex) to this new V90 format.

Tip

By the time this book is published, most ISPs and OSPs should support the faster modems – but it's worth checking!

However, these faster modems do not offer true 56Kbps throughput. This speed is only reached when downloading material. Moreover the quality of the telephone connection is crucial. If there is any 'noise on the line' your transfer speed will drop to 46Kbps, 33.6Kbps or 31.2Kbps or lower!

Modem costs for reputable makes such as Hayes, Motorola, Pace and 3Com range from £40 to £90.

ISDN lines

ISDN lines provide the fastest link readily available to the home, business and education in the UK. ISDN transmits digital information down existing telephone lines, achieving speeds of between 64Kbps and 128Kbps. It is virtually error free and can be used to transmit voice.

You need a special telephone connection in order to use ISDN. This system can only be used to access the internet if your provider (ISP or OSP) supports it. Most of the big companies, such as Demon and BT, now do so at no extra cost.

The telephone charges for ISDN are usually the same as those for the standard PSTN system. You do not need to change your own telephone number. An ISDN line will support up to 8 (or 10 if all new) telephone numbers – though not all at once.

Problems with ISDN
There are, however, some problems with ISDN for the home or small school user:

1. The cost of installation is quite expensive (about £100).

2. There is a high quarterly standing charge.

3. An ISDN adapter needs to be purchased (your standard modem is of no use). These adapters, sometimes known as **terminal adapters** (TAs), are now not much more expensive than top-of-the-range modems. However, the typical TA will only offer an average speed of 57.6Kbps. You will need a much more expensive piece of equipment called a **router** to reach the top speeds for ISDN.

When the UK pricing for ISDN becomes more realistic it will become an important means to internet access in the first decade of the next century for the home and small school user. ISDN is much cheaper on the continent.

Cable modems

A cable modem is a device that allows high speed data access to the internet through a cable television network. The cable network would typically attach to your PC and to a cable wall socket.

With several million subscribers to cable television in the UK at present this seems to be a means of access with lots of potential.

Advantages of cable modems
Cable modems have several advantages over standard telephone systems:

1. They are very fast, in fact much faster than ISDN. They are capable of receiving data at 10Mbps (10 million bits per second) and sending data at 2Mbps.

2. The line is always open (no dialling, no busy signal).

3. They do not tie up a phone line.

4. Because of their speed it will be possible to have true multimedia capability. In other words, CD-ROMs and even live video signals could be downloaded.

5. Installation is said to be easier for the small user than that of ISDN.

The future of internet communications............................

However, few UK cable companies are offering this service at present and cable modems are not generally available. It is therefore difficult to put a price on a cable internet link. But the situation could change dramatically over the next year if the price of cable modems is pegged close to that of top end modems.

Questions and answers

What does ISDN stand for?
ISDN stands for Integrated Services Digital Network. A 'basic rate' ISDN line consists of copper wiring but it carries the data in digital rather than analogue format. Connection to the internet is almost instant compared with the 30 seconds or so it takes with a modem.

What is a kilobit?
A means of measuring the speed that data travels along telephone lines (or other media). The rate of transmission is usually quoted as so many kilobits per second. Obviously the more of these you have the better! A kilobit is a thousand bits (0s or 1s, the most basic units of data in a computer).

What does modem stand for?
MOdulator/**DEM**odulator. A modem is a device that allows computers to communicate with each other over a standard telephone line. It converts (i.e. modulates) the computer's digital signal into analogue format for the journey along the telephone line and another modem at the other end changes the signal back to digital. Computers can only cope with 0s and 1s (*binary digits* – or bits for short).

What is meant by TCP/IP?
It stands for Transmission Control Protocol/Internet Protocol. This is the **protocol** (see page 11) suite used by the internet to link millions of computers worldwide. It is sometimes referred to as a stack because it consists of a pile or group of programs.

Will 'call-waiting' cause me problems when accessing the internet?
Yes! Turn it off by dialling #43# or you could lose your connection because of an incoming call. Key *43# when you have finished your internet session to reinstate 'call-waiting.'

The future

One thing is sure, internet access will become faster and cheaper. We can only hope that the internet infrastructure (the spaghetti of links that connects the thousands of servers that form the internet) can keep pace with this.

It could be that in five years' time internet connectivity is delivered to your television set through the electricity mains via one of Microsoft's own space satellites or through a new technology such as ADSL – a very high-speed service that might soon be made available by BT.

Case study

Ron is an IT teacher. He's been using computers for decades (he can remember computers before keyboards, punched tape and 8-inch floppy disks!) but he has not yet made the leap to subscribing to the internet.

He realises that he must make this jump and decides to draw up a checklist with which he can vet magazine recommendations and those of friends.

Here is the table of questions that he drew up:

Questions	internet provider 1	internet provider 2	internet provider 3	internet provider 4
Is there local phone call access? *Are engaged tones usual? Check with an internet magazine that runs service trials*				
What are the support hours? *Telephone or email?*				
What software is supplied? *Latest versions of I.E. or Netscape? Pre-configured? Extra charge?*				
What type of email is offered? *POP3 can be picked up anywhere – SMTP can't.*				
What format is the email address? *With AOL your address is user@aol.com. With Demon you have unlimited mailboxes because your address is @user.demon.co.uk. Any mailbox name can be placed before the @.*				
Are there any extra charges?				
What modem speeds are supported?				

Summary

In this chapter we have looked at the main providers of internet access and the hardware required to facilitate this. In the next chapter we will examine the educational uses of email and how to make the best use of this valuable medium.

3 Making contact by email

In this chapter you will be introduced to the following topics:

▶ *what email is*
▶ *the basic functions of email programs*
▶ *understanding email addresses*
▶ *finding email programs*
▶ *educational uses – on a LAN, and web-based mail*
▶ *internet projects and key pals*
▶ *the main elements of netiquette for email.*

For most people a major reason for connecting to the internet is the capability to send and receive electronic mail (email).

Who can I mail?

With email you can send messages to anyone on the internet who has an email address that you know. Email need not just consist of text. Most email programs allow you to send word-processed documents, spreadsheets, graphics, sound files and even video clips as **attachments**.

Email is pretty much instantaneous, most of it arriving within an hour or so. Your own email sits on the **server** of your internet provider until you log on and download it to the hard disk of your PC.

Basic email functions

Most email programs will allow you to do the following:

▷ access and read your incoming mail
▷ save your incoming mail to a **folder** or **directory**
▷ print out this mail
▷ create and send messages
▷ reply to a message received
▷ include a file in a mail message you are sending
▷ place an object such as a picture into your mail or extract one from incoming mail.

Additional useful features should include the ability:

1. to **spell check** your work
2. to create distribution lists so that one letter can be sent to more than one person
3. to maintain an **address book** of frequently contacted email correspondents whose addresses can be easily pasted into appropriate messages.

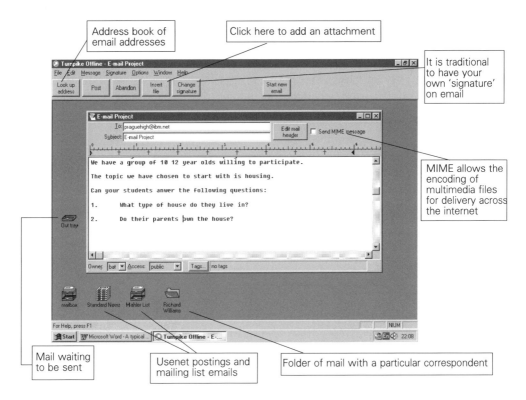

Address book of email addresses

Click here to add an attachment

It is traditional to have your own 'signature' on email

MIME allows the encoding of multimedia files for delivery across the internet

Mail waiting to be sent

Usenet postings and mailing list emails

Folder of mail with a particular correspondent

Understanding email addresses

Email addresses can be very confusing to beginners. Here is a typical example:

smith@someone.demon.co.uk

Every internet mail address has three parts:

1. a user name on the left

2. an 'at' sign – @ – in the middle

3. the address of the user's mail server on the right (the **server** means the computer on which the mail is kept).

Fig. 10. Demon's Turnpike suite is a combined email and news reading client program.

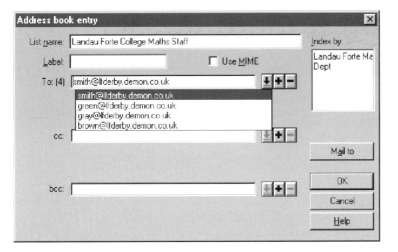

Fig. 11. A distribution list for a Maths Department. One email can be sent to all members of the department.

27

Domain names

In the example above the username is 'smith' and his/her mail is kept on the server of the Demon internet provider. 'Someone' is what we call the **nodename**. It is just a way of uniquely identifying an account with Demon.

Some companies such as AOL and Virgin Net do not use nodenames. Therefore you will find that email addresses with these companies use these formats:

smith10@aol

smith10@virgin.net.

The '10' (or some other number) is there because there is bound to be more that one 'smith' with these large companies.

Tip
It helps to read the domain from right to left in order to understand how it is structured.

An advantage of using a nodename in the address is that you can have as many user names as you wish to the left of the @ sign. This allows you to have what are known as **multiple mailboxes**. Companies such as AOL and VirginNet usually only offer 5 mailboxes per member.

Let's take another look at our original example:

smith@someone.demon.co.uk

The element to the right of the @ is what we call the **domain name,** in this case 'demon.co.uk'.

Starting from the extreme right the 'uk' clearly tell us the country of origin of the address. Note: US addresses do not have country codes. The 'co' tells us that this a non-US company (US companies have 'com' in their address instead of 'co'); 'demon' is obviously the name of the ISP and 'someone' the nodename uniquely identifying this specific account.

The domain names system

The elements of the domain name have been systematised by international agreement.

Below is a basic list of these elements in use today.

edu	US educational/university site
com	US commercial site
co	non-US commercial site
gov	government site
net	network administrative organisation
mil	military site
org	organisations (usually non-profit-making)
int	international organisation
ac	non-US educational/university site
uk	UK site
fr	French site

Most other countries now have their own codes (de Germany, ne Netherlands, hk Hong Kong, ru Russia and so on).

Possible new abbreviations

In the near future a further batch of abbreviations might be available. The following have been suggested but not approved:

nom	private individual's site
store	internet shopping site
firm	firms and businesses
web	site emphasising activities related to the web
arts	site for cultural and entertainment activities
rec	site for recreational activities
info	site for those providing information services

Finding email programs

There are plenty of good email programs available. Some come in the integrated packages supplied by service providers such as in Demon's Turnpike suite or the AOL bundle. These are on the whole excellent products, though in the case of Demon you do have to pay extra for the software. With Virgin Net there is no extra charge.

Fig. 12. Pegasus Mail has an easy to use interface and it's free on many magazine cover disks. Plus there's lots of help available to set it up!

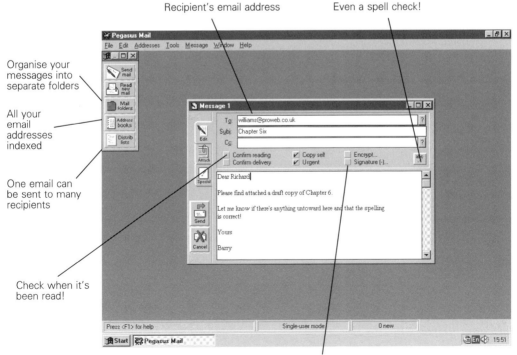

Recipient's email address

Even a spell check!

Organise your messages into separate folders

All your email addresses indexed

One email can be sent to many recipients

Check when it's been read!

Choose your signature according to your mood

29

Email on a school local area network (LAN)................

Free email programs

However, there is some very good news in that there are some totally free independent email packages. The well-known ones include:

▷ Pegasus Mail

▷ Eudora Lite (the fuller priced version is called Eudora Pro).

Both can be easily networked for a school local area network (using Novell or Windows NT). In this way all staff and students can have their own email accounts.

Pegasus Mail and Eudora Lite can be obtained from several sources (see addresses in the Appendix). They can be downloaded:

1. through a web browser such as Netscape or Microsoft Internet Explorer (very easy) or

2. through FTP (usually quicker to download but not so easy to use).

Once online, you fire up your browser and find the closest sites to you by carrying out a search for the program that interests you, for example using AltaVista or Yahoo.

Electronic mail on a school local area network (LAN)

Email for teachers

Email will become a vital tool in keeping teachers well informed in the context of a busy school. It can be used to inform teachers of:

▷ the content of daily/weekly briefings
▷ progress of individual students (particularly when there is an imminent parents' consultation meeting)
▷ events inside and outside the school
▷ meetings, agendas and minutes of meetings.

After initial training staff quickly latch onto to the use of email. However, it is important that staff:

1. log on frequently to the system, at least daily
2. deal with their mail swiftly, deleting as much as possible
3. have good access to IT equipment, with at least one PC per work room or a ratio of one machine to five teachers.

Email for students

For students email on a LAN has limited uses. Email is best granted for specific projects. **Acceptable use policies** (see Chapter 7) and contracts need to be issued and complied with.

▷ Email between school students in the same building can be a stupendous time-waster and can involve an enormous amount of administrative effort due to misuse and downright abuse.

▷ If email is to be made available to large numbers of students a great deal of prior training and preparation is needed.

Moreover, the IT staff must have appropriate tools for controlling it. These tools should:

1. allow student mail to be sent sometime after it has been written

2. allow mail boxes to be scanned for unsuitable material

3. restrict access to certain times of the day.

From personal experience we would urge caution when considering open access to email for school students.

Perhaps in a few years' time this issue will cease to be relevant once many students have accounts at home.

Web-based mail

The government has proposed that all secondary students should have their own mailboxes within the next few years. Several internet-based companies have come up with proposals to offer individuals free mailboxes for life though web-based mail.

Many schools might find this a preferable option to managing accounts themselves. Moreover, companies offering these mailboxes offer to restrict mailings to known email addresses and to filter out junk mail and stop in-coming mail from sites put forward by their teachers.

Points to consider

However, the following points need consideration:

1. Web-based email is very slow to use and needs a live connection to the internet.

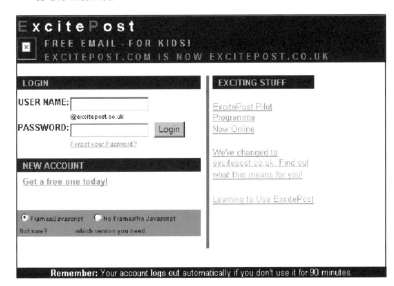

Fig. 13. ExcitePost offers free email accounts for life to every school student and teacher in the land.

Email projects

2. It can take some time to set up each account.

3. If students have access from web mail to their user areas on the LAN it is difficult to control what is being downloaded. For example, computer viruses could be introduced onto the LAN.

4. Advertising is placed on students' mail screens and might be added to their actual emails in the future.

Educational uses of email across the internet

Email projects between schools have been popular for several years. They are relatively easy to set up but do require a lot of commitment on both sides if they are to be successful.

Here we will list some examples of projects that have been carried out by both teachers and students in the author's school and by teachers elsewhere in the UK.

Teachers' projects

Teachers discussing with other teachers:

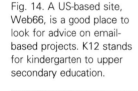
Fig. 14. A US-based site, Web66, is a good place to look for advice on email-based projects. K12 stands for kindergarten to upper secondary education.

▷ educational issues – comparing roles and systems

▷ lesson plans

▷ ideas, resources and sources of teaching materials

▷ the implementation of new syllabuses

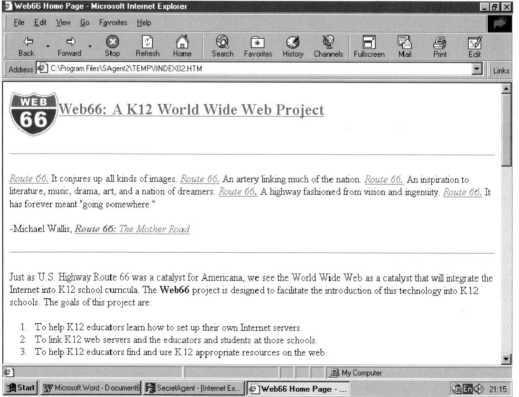

▷ support issues for courses at GCSE or A level

▷ job exchanges

▷ support for heads, deputies, middle managers and newly qualified staff.

Students' projects

Students involved with students in other institutions:

▷ setting up internet key-pal links in English or a modern foreign language

▷ setting up work experience in another EU country

▷ setting up student exchanges

▷ encouraging new users of email by mailing them when they are online

▷ acting as Santa Claus when replying to emails from primary school pupils

▷ joint projects on a range of topics. Examples could include:

> describing each other's families
> describing their school systems
> describing their interests in sport
> describing 'what they do' on their holidays
> producing brochures/guides to home towns in a modern
>   foreign language
> sharing weather data
> discussing political systems
> investigating life in World War Two across several European
>   countries.

Sources of project ideas

There are several ways of finding information about projects:

1. There are web sites that keep details of such projects such as Research Machines' Internet for Learning site, BT's Campus World or Web66 (see addresses in the Appendix).

2. There are mailing lists such as uk-education and Web66 (more details in Chapter 5).

3. You could subscribe to an educational newsgroup where projects are often advertised. Newsgroups are dealt with in Chapter 4.

Key-pal contacts

Key-pal links (the computer term for pen pals!) can be found by contacting the same sources as above. In addition, you could mail suitable schools directly. Several web sites contain long lists of school email addresses. Both Research Machines Internet for Learning (Netpals at Eduweb) and Web66 have catalogues of such addresses.

Netiquette . . . .

Planning for projects

Before starting an email project it is a good idea to plan out exactly what is involved. Work to a timetable of events with the partner institution(s). It is not a good idea for such a project to be left open-ended. If it is, things will drift and one side at least will lose interest.

The following points are also worth considering:

(a) Try and make personal contact with the teacher-leaders involved, by telephone or even regular mail. Some of the best projects have involved the main organisers meeting face to face.

(b) Give your students a time frame. Ensure that they write regularly.

(c) Teachers (or technical staff) need to check the content of incoming and outgoing mail for any inappropriate material.

(d) Expect disappointments, lack of replies and interest, and technical problems (especially with projects with schools in Eastern Europe!).

(e) Teachers and staff need to be aware of netiquette (see below).

(f) Students need to learn that not everyone on the internet is as they seem (see Chapter 7).

Netiquette

By this strange term we mean the 'rules' by which you should communicate with other email and usenet users. There are many sites that contain documents on netiquette, as a search in AltaVista or Yahoo will reveal. Below we summarise the main conventions.

1. Never send a message in capital letters. Firstly it is hard to read and secondly it is the internet equivalent of SHOUTING.

2. When replying to messages do not include the entire contents in your reply unless the original was very short.

3. Do not reply to a letter without quoting or paraphrasing *something* from the original.

4. Do not send messages with lines longer than 70 characters. Some mail programs can mutilate your exquisite prose. Check your mail program set-up.

5. Email is not secure. It is possible for it to be read by someone else (but not likely). Very sensitive material should only be sent by email if it is encrypted in some way. You might wish to investigate the use of a well-known free encryption program such as Pretty Good Privacy (PGP).

6. Check the 'To' and 'cc' lines of your message. Are you *sure* you want the message to go there?

7. Remember that no one can hear the tone of your voice. Use emoticons or smileys (see below). For emphasis you can use capitals, asterisks or exclamation marks.

8. If you have a signature file, keep it short and no more than 5 lines in depth.

9. Do not just send a reply to a message with a 'Me too' or 'I don't know'. You do not have to reply to every message sent to you.

10. In certain situations use acronyms – they save typing but can be irritating if they are obscure or used excessively.

Smileys or emoticons

These can add some humour to letters, though few are actually used in normal email. Try these:

happy   :-)   sad   :-(

Once again, a full list of smileys (including some very dubious ones) can be obtained by carrying out a search in Yahoo! or AltaVista.

Common acronyms for email use

Here are some of the most commonly used acronyms. Use sparingly!

ASAP	as soon as possible
BTW	by the way
FWIW	for what it's worth
FYI	for your information
HTH	hope this helps
IAE	in any event
IMHO	in my humble opinion
IOW	in other words
NRN	no reply necessary
OTOH	on the other hand
ROTFL	rolling on the floor laughing
RTFM	read the 'flipping' manual
SITD	still in the dark
TIA	thanks in advance

Case study

Marc wants to set up an email link between his top primary class and a similar class in the USA. He has chosen the USA because there will be few language problems involved.

He realises that there must be a focus to this venture and chooses a topic that he knows has worked well elsewhere. Students are to compare the types of houses they live in and describe the facilities available locally.

Questions and answers ···

Marc accesses the *E-pals* internet site (see Appendix) and finds a match with a Florida school (several of his students had been there!). He decides that the project will last eight weeks – this is about the right length to keep the interest of his class. Initially both schools exchange information by the standard postal system. This package contains photographs, letters, newsletters and audiotapes.

Questions and answers

What is a server?
A computer on a network that serves other computers, e.g. a web server holds web pages and software.

What is client software?
A program that allows access to information across a network. Web browsers and ftp programs allow you to access data on web and ftp servers.

What is a LAN?
LAN stands for Local Area Network. This is a computer network usually in one building or one site such as a school.

Fig. 15. The Bigfoot search engine for email addresses.

What is data encryption?
It means encoding data so that it is difficult for outsiders to read when it is transmitted between two computers or across a network. A

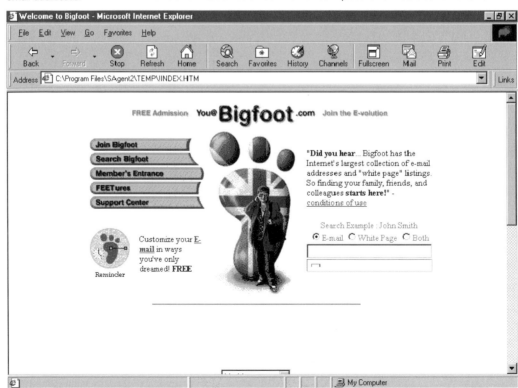

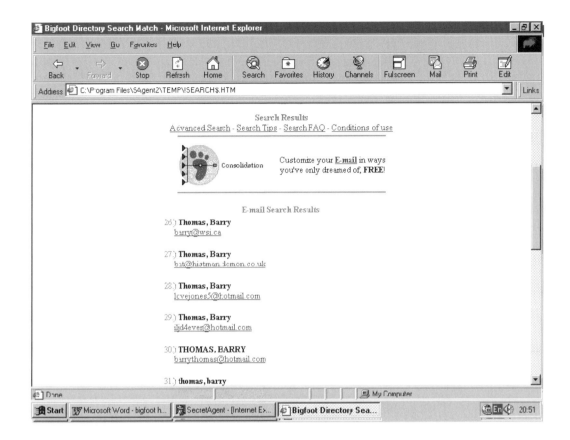

Fig. 16. The results of a search in Bigfoot for Barry Thomas's email addresses.

decoding program is needed on the receiving computer. Modern computers make powerful data encryption very easy.

How do I find out other people's email addresses?
As there is no single equivalent to a telephone directory on the internet this can be difficult. There are various options that you can try:

▷ Access www.bigfoot.co.uk, which is more UK-focused than most online email address directories.

▷ If you know the person's internet provider, you can email the company's postmaster, for example

    postmaster@demon.net

for Demon accounts.

▷ Try searching for the name in AltaVista.

What is an 'attachment'?
An **attachment** is a file that is sent with an email message. This could be anything from a word-processed document to a spreadsheet file or a graphics file. Email can only cope with simple text files. Your mail program usually encodes the attached files.

37

Summary ·

What is a signature?
A short piece of standard text which you can place at the bottom of your emails. It should not be more than 4 or 5 lines long (see netiquette). You might include your email address, or the address of your home page (if you have one). It has become a tradition to include a favourite quote or saying in your signature though this is optional and many users of email hate them!

Summary

In this chapter we have looked at the basic features of email packages, the educational uses of email including key-pal links and class projects, how you can find these projects and plan them. We finished by looking at some aspects of netiquette.

In the next chapter we will see how usenet news can be used in the classroom. We will also examine how mailing lists can help keep teachers up to date with educational issues.

4 Usenet – a very useful resource

In this chapter you will be introduced to the following topics:

▶ *what is usenet*
▶ *how newsgroups are organised*
▶ *the main educational newsgroups*
▶ *how to subscribe to newsgroups*
▶ *how to read and reply to newsgroups*
▶ *the role of the newbie and dangers to students on newsgroups*
▶ *how to find past discussions on usenet.*

What is usenet?

Newsgroups on the internet do not have much to do with news. They are really discussion groups to which participants post their messages. The messages can be read by all readers of the newsgroup. Any reader of the newsgroup can reply either publicly or privately by email to the poster.

Newsgroups are an extremely useful means of exchanging ideas between teachers and getting technical and curriculum questions answered or discussed.

Fig. 17. A typical posting to uk.education.teachers.

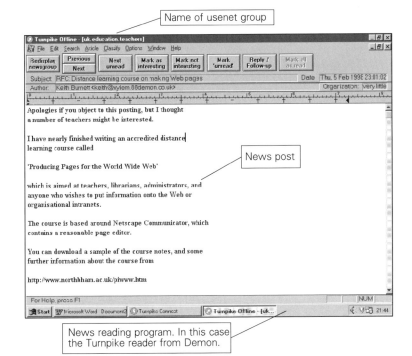

Name of usenet group

News post

News reading program. In this case the Turnpike reader from Demon.

Newsgroups

Since email is used to take part in newsgroup discussion, it is possible to post messages with attachments in the form of photographs, sound or video clips. This is not popular in most newsgroups because these files take time to download and will force up users' telephone bills.

Usenet originated from the days of computer bulletin boards. Usenet is an abbreviation of Users' Network but it is not actually a computer network or even part of the internet. It consists of a huge mass of newsgroups that are sent around the world by computers known as **news servers**. These servers exchange information so that each one carries a copy of the most recent messages.

Usenet actually predates the internet but most of the transfer of news takes place through it. However, it is possible to access the usenet newsgroups through a dial-up connection to a local bulletin board. These have declined in popularity since the growth of the world wide web.

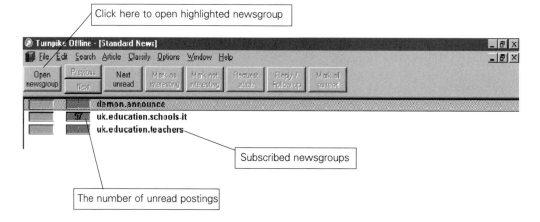

Fig.18. Subscribed newsgroups in a typical newsreader.

How newsgroups are organised

Newsgroups are organised **hierarchically**. The widest group appears first in the name, and is normally followed by a number of subgroups. The name of each group is separated from its parent and subgroup by a full stop. Take this example:

alt.education.email-project

▷ *alt* is a major subject group

▷ *education* is a sub group

▷ *email project* is the specific area of interest of this group.

When usenet began, the major news categories were:

comp	computer science related topics
news	concerned with the news network and news software
rec	concerned with hobbies, arts and recreational interests

sci	scientific research and applications
soc	social issues
talk	debate on controversial issues
misc	anything that does not fit into the above!

Since the early days of the internet other major subject groups have been added such as:

alt	massive number of alternative discussion groups – on every subject under the sun from New Age to alternative medicine (many of the unpleasant sex groups are in this category; companies such as Research Machines block out groups like this)
biz	business
K12	Kindergarten to Grade 12 – contains a large number of US-based educational discussion groups.

Other top-level categories also exist now concerning specific countries. There are, for example, a large number of UK groups.

To date well over 30,000 groups exist, with new ones being formed daily. It is possible for servers to have local groups that can be restricted to local users though they can be shared with other news servers.

Educational groups

UK newsgroups

The number of UK newsgroups has grown over the last few years. The main discussion group is

> uk.education.schools

This receives a large number of postings during term time. IT specialists will want to join

> uk.education.schools-it

which is a good place to find advice. It does, however, get bogged down in 'platform wars' – arguments between PC and Acorn users!

Both groups contain some veteran posters and are friendly to new posters as long as the basics of netiquette are observed. Other useful newsgroups include:

> uk.education.16plus
> uk.education.home-education
> uk.education.maths
> uk.education.misc
> uk.education.schools
> uk.education.schools-it
> uk.education.staffroom
> uk.education.teachers

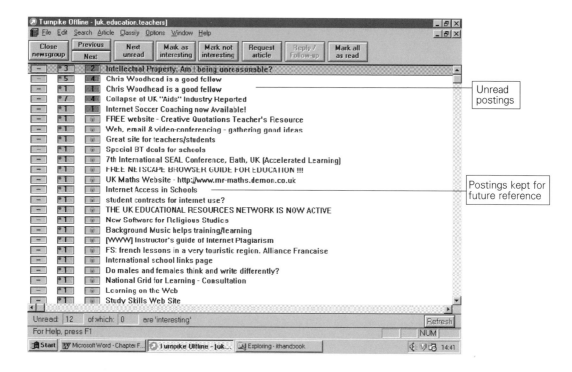

Fig. 19. Sample postings to the uk.education.teachers newsgroup.

K12 groups

The K12 groups are US-based but are read by educationalists throughout the world. For beginners this one is worth trying:

K12.teacher

IT teachers might start with

K12.comp.literacy.

As in all newsgroups, the quality and quantity of the postings can vary considerably. At the end of the day it is all down to their various members. It is probably a good idea to dip into these groups from time to time:

K12.chat.elementary	K12.ed.music
K12.chat.junior	K12.ed.science
K12.chat.senior	K12.ed.soc-studies
K12.chat.teacher	K12.ed.tech
K12.ed.art	K12.lang.francais
K12.ed.business	K12.lang.russian
K12.ed.comp.literacy	K12.news
K12.ed.math	

How to subscribe to a newsgroup

To receive postings from newsgroups you have to **subscribe** or join them. This is free and is not difficult to carry out. You don't have to part with any personal information.

You can access newsgroups through browsers such as Netscape but specialised **news reading** software is easier to use and usually has more facilities. Most ISPs supply their own version, though free readers can be downloaded from internet sites. One of the popular ones is Free Agent. It often features on free magazine cover disks.

The first thing you need to do is download the full list of groups available to you from your ISP. Some ISPs do not give you access to all newsgroups available, on the grounds of either censorship or cost.

Most readers allow you to read **offline** (not being connected to the internet). You should plump for one of these to keep down your phone bill.

Fig. 20. Downloading a complete list of newsgroups.

Click on News when Outlook Express loads for the first time and you will see this message

Outlook Express is bundled with Internet Explorer 4

43

Reading news

This is just like reading email. Posts are sorted by subject topic. A reply to a posting can start a **thread**, a term which describes a list of related replies. You can normally 'view thread' as well as the individual messages.

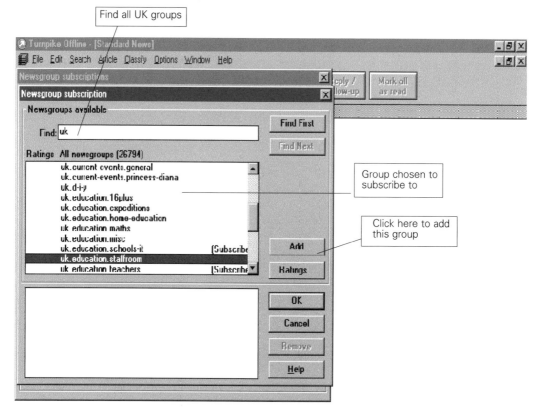

Fig. 21. Subscribing to a UK education newsgroup from a full list of newsgroups

Fig. 22. An extract from 'uk.education.schools-it' showing a thread on the same topic.

Replying to news

Whatever your news-reading software, you usually have the options of

1. replying to the newsgroup as a whole

2. replying directly to an individual subscriber by private email.

In the posting in Figure 23 we replied to the sender by private email.

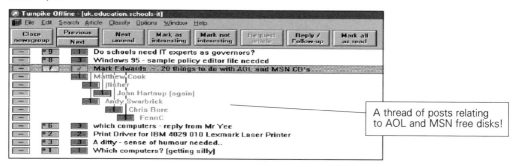

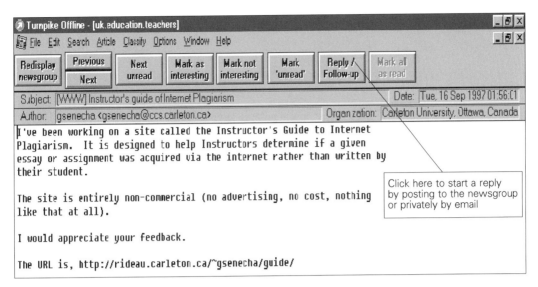

You are a newbie!

At this stage you are a newbie (yes, a terrible term!). Jumping in without being aware of the conventions of the group can lead to you being **flamed** (bombarded with more or less hostile messages).

Before getting involved in newsgroup discussion it is best to get a feel for the group for several weeks by reading posts and the replies. This is known as **lurking**, and is a perfectly respectable activity.

It is also a very good idea to get hold of the FAQ for the group. FAQ is the universally accepted acronym for 'frequently asked questions'. It refers to a list of standard questions about the group, with standard answers to guide you. The FAQ should give you some idea of the rules

Fig. 23. A posting advertising a paper on internet plagiarism.

Fig. 24. The author's reply by email.

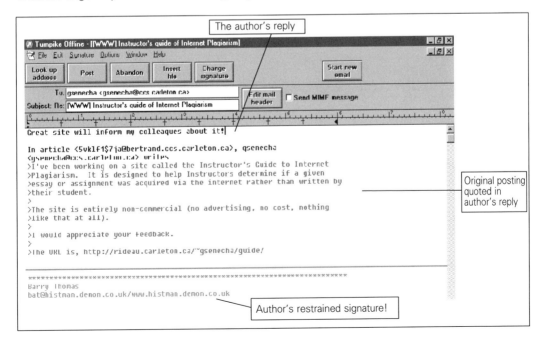

Doing a newsgroup search..

of the group. It should prevent you from asking something that regularly appears in the group and is regularly answered.

Dangers to students

It need hardly be said that students should only enter these groups with care and should never post their full names, addresses and telephone numbers.

Finding previous discussions

Before posing a question on usenet it is usually a good idea to check whether the topic has been discussed sometime in the near past. Of course, this might also be noted in the FAQ(s) for the particular group(s) that you are intending to post to. Another way of finding out is to do a search.

Dejanews

Fig. 25. Dejanews is the best search engine to track down discussions on usenet.

A good place to do a newsgroup search is the Dejanews site. This popular site maintains an enormous database of discussions in a vast number of newsgroups. This is also a good place to find groups that might interest you, as you cannot be sure that your internet provider gives you a full feed of newsgroups.

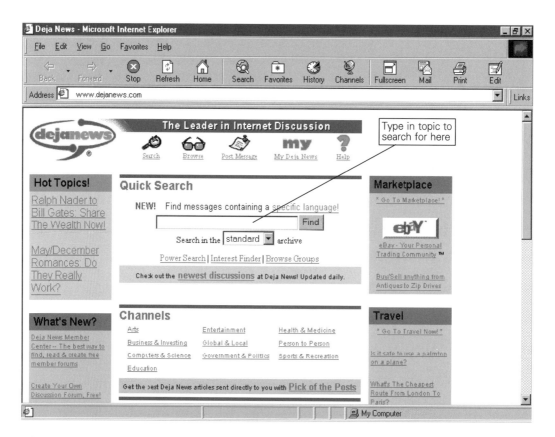

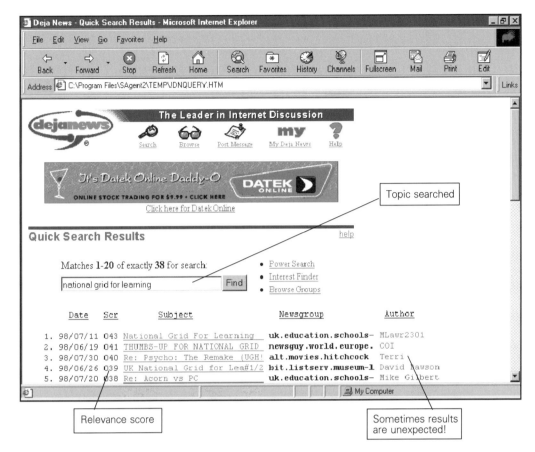

Fig. 26. Dejanews result of a search for the National Grid for Learning. Sometimes bizarre results are delivered! Remember, the results are not compiled by humans beings, but electronically by computers.

Questions and answers

What is a bulletin board?
A computer bulletin board works in the same way as a notice board in your home or office. You just stick notices on to it for others to read. The computer bulletin board messages are posted and replied to by means of email.

What is meant by flaming?
Flaming is when a poster to a newsgroup is verbally attacked by another user (or users) for breaking the rules of netiquette or making what is regarded as an unreasonable statement.

What is CIX?
CIX stands for Compulink Information Exchange. It was an early UK forum for online discussion, which began in 1988. It is still in existence and hosts several educational discussion areas. It originally operated solely as a bulletin board (see above).

Where do I find FAQs?

1. In the newsgroup itself. In most groups FAQs are posted once a month.

2. A search in Yahoo! or AltaVista will give you the location of thousands of FAQs.

3. Post a request for the FAQs in the newsgroup itself!

The future of newsgroups

The number of newsgroups will continue to multiply rapidly on usenet. However, similar discussion groups have been available on CIX for some time and will develop on the government's National Grid for Learning site (see Appendix). Hopefully these will be subject-based or deal with wider issues. Already there are discussion groups for school managers, for example.

In the future, this text-based system will probably be replaced by multimedia elements such as photographs, video clips and sound. However, we will need a faster internet to support this! No doubt this is on the way.

Case studies

Windows 95 problems

Amanda Q is network manager of a school's network. She is having problems with students altering the settings of Windows 95. She decides to post a request for help on the uk.education.it-schools newsgroup that often deals with cries for help like this.

Luckily another subscriber Mark T. has the answer, having experienced the same problem. He offers to email Amanda with several answers to her problem.

French contacts wanted

Tim is a teacher of modern foreign languages. He is looking for a contact with a French school teacher so that his students can start up a key-pal project with French youngsters. He posts his request to:

K12.language.francais.

Luckily a teacher from Lyons sees his message and emails Tim with the addresses of suitable French students.

Summary

In this chapter we have examined how usenet is organised, looked at the main educational groups and how to subscribe, contribute and leave them. We have also addressed some of the problems that can be encountered when using them.

In the next chapter we will discover how educationalists can make the best use of mailing lists.

5 Want some mail? Join a mailing list!

In this chapter you will be introduced to the following topics:

▶ *why you might want to join mailing lists*
▶ *what is a listserver*
▶ *how to find useful lists*
▶ *how to join and leave a list*
▶ *advice on using lists sensibly*
▶ *how to access archives of postings*
▶ *how set up your own list.*

. . . .

Joining a mailing list

Just as usenet involves the use of email to post messages, another service is available on the internet which also depends on email. This is the **mailing list**.

Subscribing

You **subscribe** to a mailing list, rather like you subscribe to a newsgroup. You then receive regular information by email about the

Fig. 27. A typical posting to the 'uk-schools' list.

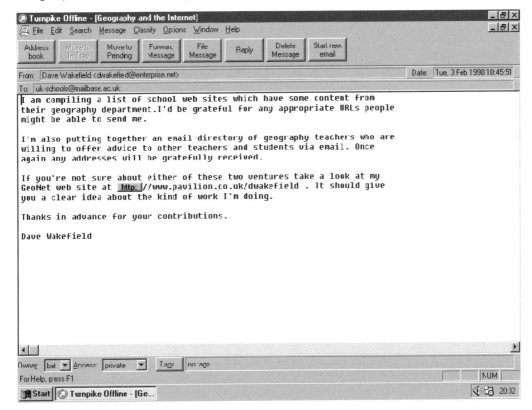

Useful lists

subject that mailing list is concerned with.

The electronic mail is sent to you automatically by a **listserver** computer (see below). You will continue to receive this email until you **unsubscribe.** The audience for mailing lists is usually smaller and more specialist than that for usenet.

Why join a mailing list?

1. It allows you to share information, ideas and knowledge with fellow professionals in the same subject area.

2. You can engage in scholarly discussion.

3. You can exchange educational news and ideas across the globe.

4. It's easy to use and is free.

5. Some list services offer a high level of support.

What is a listserver?

A listserver is a robot computer. It is often based at a university where it manages all the email traffic. The listserver performs two jobs:

▷ It keeps a list of names and addresses of members who have subscribed.

▷ It receives all email messages sent to the list and then 'bounces' them out to all the other members of the list. Everybody on the list receives a copy of all messages sent to the list.

Many lists are **moderated**. This means that before messages are sent out the moderator (a real live person) can weed out anything they consider unsuitable or 'off-topic'.

Finding useful lists

UK lists

The main UK educational lists are maintained at the Mailbase at Newcastle University. Mailbase hosts over 1,800 lists and has 126,000 subscribing members.

The best educational UK lists to subscribe to are:

uk-schools (primary and secondary)

uk-colleges (post 16).

The National Grid for Learning site hosts several lists including those for SENCOs and senior management staff. A search through Yahoo!

revealed 59 references to educational mailing lists.

Other lists

There are various search engines on the web you can use to find suitable listservers. Try visiting and using these search engines:

▷ www.tile.com
▷ The Liszt site www.liszt.com
▷ The Publicly Accessible Mailing Lists site www.neosoft.com
▷ The Web66 site (which has its own US-based listserver) http://web66.coled.umn.edu/

How to manage your mailing lists

Most mailing lists are managed by automatic software packages such as:

▷ Listserv
▷ MajorDomo
▷ almanac.

These accept similar commands.

Fig. 28. Our search in Yahoo! for education mailing lists yielded 59 results.

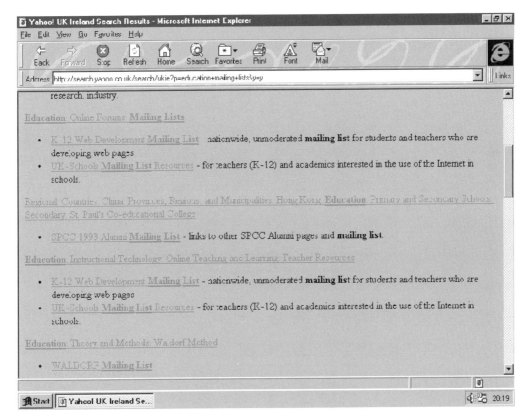

Finding mailing lists on the internet

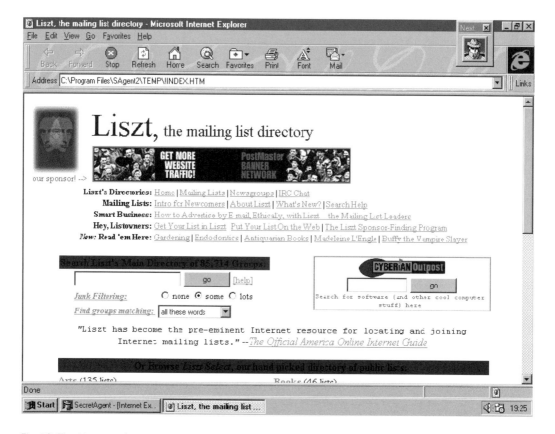

Fig. 29. The Liszt search engine for mailing lists.

Fig. 30. The Publicly Accessible Mailing Lists site.

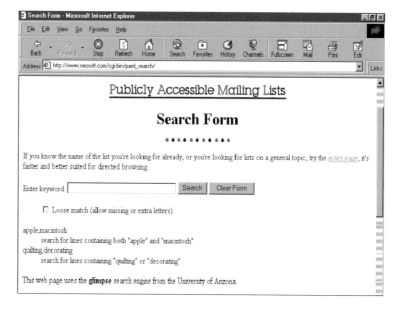

Contacting your listserver

Most listservers have two main email addresses for you to contact:

1. the address to send commands to (for example, to subscribe or leave the list)

2. the address to send your message or comment to other list members.

Example: the 'uk-schools' list

1. You send your commands to: mailbase@mailbase.ac.uk'.

2. You send messages to list-members to: uk-schools@mailbase.ac.uk'.

Subscribing to lists

Suppose you want to subscribe to a mailing list managed by one of these automatic packages. You must first send a specially framed message to a stipulated address on the computer that runs the list.

The address is often the name of the program managing the list. For example, to subscribe to 'uk-schools' you first need to load your email program. Then, in the 'to' part of the program you should type:

mailbase@mailbase.ac.uk

Fig. 31. Details of the 'uk-schools' list at www.mailbase.ac.uk.

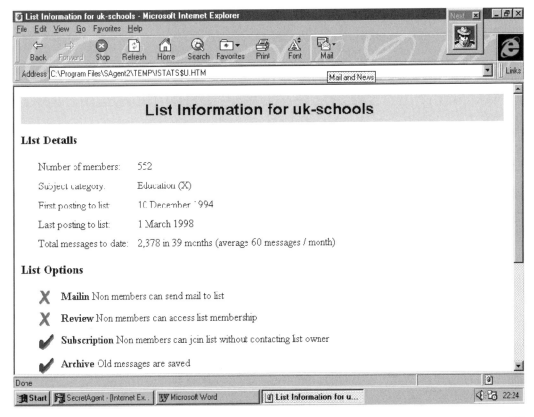

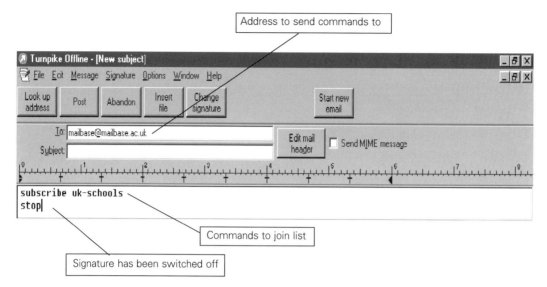

Address to send commands to

Commands to join list

Signature has been switched off

Fig. 32. Subscribing to 'uk-schools'. *Note*: the Subject line has been intentionally left blank.

In the letter part of the program type:

> subscribe uk-schools yourfirstname yourlastname

See Figure 32.

The listserver software takes your email address from your message header.

After subscribing you will usually be sent confirmation of your acceptance to the list, and instructions on how to manage your account. Make sure you do not delete these!

Unsubscribing

To leave the 'uk-school' list, type the following in the letter part of the program:

> unsubscribe uk-schools

Suspending and resuming mailings

If you are going on holiday for a few weeks you may wish to suspend your account. Once again you should mail your command to mailbase@mailbase.ac.uk. In this case type:

> suspend all

To resume your mail send a message to mailbase with the request:

> resume all

Tip! It is best to avoid writing anything else in your message. Do not type your name. Switch off your signature if you can. Some listserver systems prefer you to type 'stop' on a new line after your command.

Guidelines for mailing to lists

When sending messages to a list you need to be aware that it will be read by a variety of readers and on a variety of computers. The message you send needs to be of benefit to other members of the list.

You need to be aware of the following points:

1. Make sure that you send commands to the right address.

2. Suspend your mail when going on holiday (for more than 2 weeks).

3. Keep messages relevant to the subject of the list.

4. Don't flame – in other words verbally attack another list member.

5. Don't forward private mail to the list without permission.

6. Don't quote the entire message in your reply. Snip out as much as you can without losing the sense of the reply.

7. Don't solicit commercial business or send promotional materials to the list.

8. Keep your lines short, your messages brief and your signatures short.

9. Don't send private mail by mistake to the list. A contributor to the Fortean Times list inadvertently sent a missive about a nasty breast infection to the entire list!

Fig. 33. The Mailbase site contains a wealth of information about mailing lists.

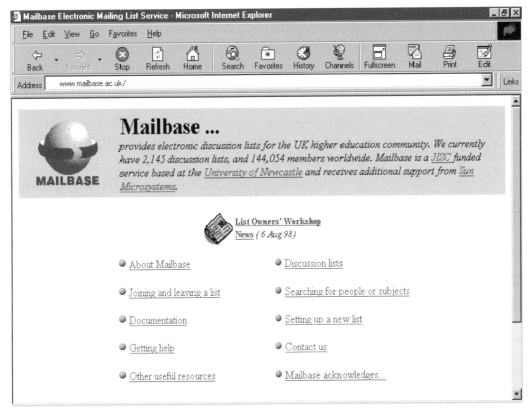

Setting up your own list ....

Archives of postings

Most lists have **archives** (back copies) of postings available to members, or even the general public. The archives for the 'open' lists at Mailbase, for example, can be read through a web browser at the Mailbase web site. Other lists will allow you to receive archived material through email.

To investigate this useful facility, contact the list owner. You will be given their name when you first tender your subscription.

Setting up your own mailing list

How about setting up your own list for a group of schools, or for a specific curriculum topic? All this is possible. Some web servers will host your list and provide the software to send out the emails to list members.

Fig. 34. The Onelist site (www.onelist.com) is a good place to find lists and to start your own.

Mailbase is a good place to try if you are in further education. Onelist hosts hundreds of lists.

The software company L-Soft wrote the original listserv software and has several useful manuals which you can download free.

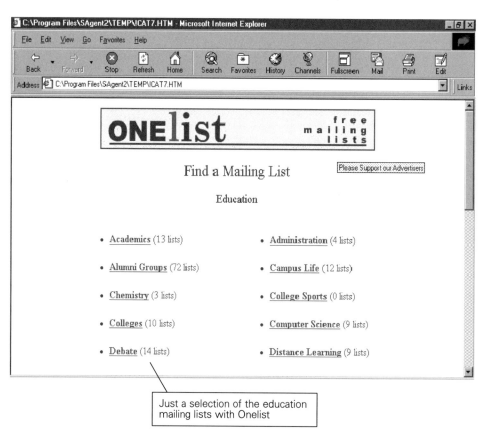

Just a selection of the education mailing lists with Onelist

Questions and answers

What is meant by 'traffic' in mailing lists?
Traffic refers to the average amount of postings to the list per day. Some lists have heavy traffic which means that you might receive in excess of 30 postings a day. This is rather a lot to read at the end of a school day. At present, uk-school receives about 60 postings a month, though it could grow!

What is the difference between the commands 'join' and 'subscribe'?
None. Most listservers will accept either. You are usually mailed a list of basic commands by your listserver when you subscribe to a list. If not, they can usually be easily downloaded from the listserver site.

Why do you need to suspend your list membership when you are on holiday?
Some ISPs will bounce back undelivered mail to the listserver if it is not delivered within a week or so. This is because your mail is occupying space on their computers. Your listserver provider will not find all this rejected mail amusing!

What is a MajorDomo?
It's nothing to do with the army. MajorDomo is a list managing system used by many servers. It is used as an alternative to the listserv software developed by L-Soft.

What is an 'open' list?
This is a list that anyone can join. To join a restricted or closed list you usually need to have an invitation.

Case study

Jules and Kath are Special Needs tutors in a large comprehensive school. They want to keep abreast of developments in this area, especially in regard to dyslexia.

Their IT co-ordinator informs them that BECTA has a list for SENCOs. He points them in the direction of the National Grid for Learning site (see Appendix) where there is a link to the SENCOs' mailing list.

Almost immediately Jules and Kath receive daily postings on a whole range of Special Needs topics.

After a few weeks of **lurking** they ask for help on dyslexia.

Summary

In this chapter we have looked at the uses of mailing lists and how to join, participate in and leave them. In the next chapter we will review in detail the world wide web – which, after email, is the most used area of the internet.

6 Explore the world wide web from your armchair

In this chapter you will be introduced to the following topics:

▶ *web browsers and how to use them*
▶ *how to read internet addresses*
▶ *using the major search engines and directories (including search programs for school students)*
▶ *getting the best out of search engines*
▶ *general tips on surfing the web.*

. . . .

The world wide web is probably the most used part of the internet after electronic mail. For many it is the most exciting part of the internet, containing millions of pages of text and graphics. These pages can be connected to other pages, which may be lodged on computers anywhere in the world.

Browsing the web

In order to view the world wide web (web for short) you need to use a program known as a **browser**. The two most popular browsers come from:

▷ Netscape (the first on the market) – Netscape Communicator
▷ Microsoft Internet Explorer (version 5 available mid-1999).

They are very similar in what they do and how they do it, and it won't make very much difference which one you use. Both are free to educational users. The examples in this book are from Microsoft's Internet Explorer versions 3 and 4.

▷ To view new web pages you need to have a live connection to the internet.
▷ Pages that you have already viewed can be saved to your hard drive as **cache** files. It is possible to read these pages with specialised cache reading software such as Secret Agent (from http://www.ariel.co.uk).

Web pages can come in almost endless varieties. They can contain text, pictures, sound or interactive elements. Most contain links to other pages. These links are known as **hypertext links** (see Figure 36).

Key features of a browser

These can be seen in Figure 37. The main features of Microsoft's browser, Internet Explorer, are:

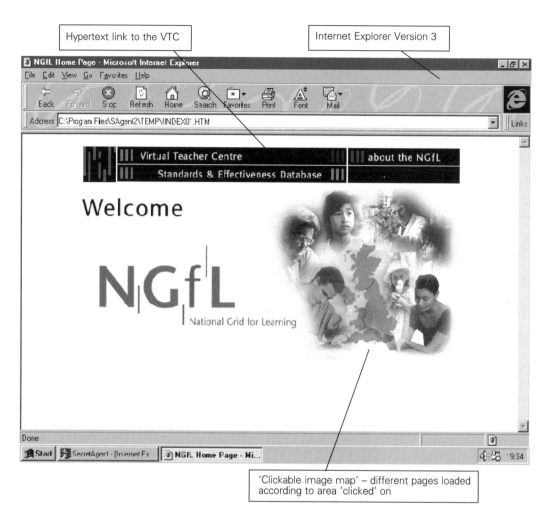

'Clickable image map' – different pages loaded according to area 'clicked' on

Fig. 36. The opening web page of the National Grid for Learning site, showing hypertext links.

▷ an address box, which shows the address of the web page you are viewing

▷ a row of icons across the top, which you can click when you want to deal with your email, view favourite web sites, print out a web page, and so on.

Understanding web addresses

All web sites have a unique address known as their **URL**. This is short for **uniform resource locator**.

Web addresses

Web sites are always prefixed with the letters:

http://

The 'http' stands for **hypertext transport protocol**. Let's look at an imaginary URL and identify its various constituents:

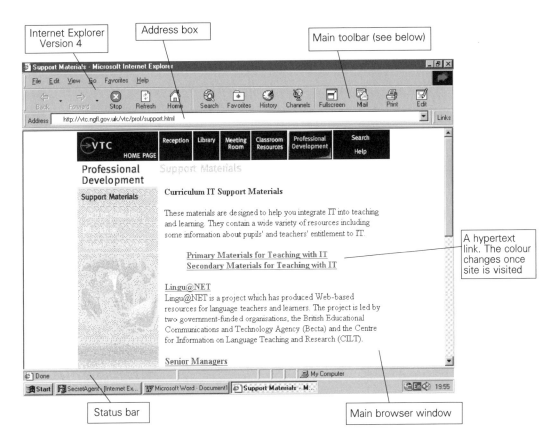

Fig 37. Internet Explorer version 4 – main features.

Button	Function
Back	Last web page(s) viewed
Forward	Returns to page(s) you were viewing before clicking on Back
Stop	Stops data transfer over the internet
Refresh	Reloads current page. Handy if transfer has been interrupted
Home	Takes you to your start page. You can set this yourself
Search	Takes you to internet search programs
Favorites	The place to bookmark your favourite sites
Font	Alters font size of current page
History	Shows sites visited recently
Channels	Lists channels subscribed to; data sent to you from web site
Fullscreen	Maximises screen and then returns it to standard setting
Mail	Takes you to inbuilt Mail and News features
Print	Prints current page
Edit	Takes you to *Front Page* editor if program is installed

Domain naming

The extension '.html' denotes that this is an html file.

FTP sites

Not all addresses on the internet start with http:// For example, FTP sites begin with

ftp://

FTP sites are servers that hold files and programs that can be downloaded to your hard disk (given the necessary permissions) using Internet Explorer, other browsers or specialised software.

Usenet servers

Usenet servers are usually identified by the word:

news:

Gopher servers

Gopher was an older system for cataloguing materials on the internet. Gopher servers are identified by:

gopher:

You probably will not come across these often.

Internet domain naming

Before reading what follows, you might wish to refer to the section on email-naming conventions in Chapter 3, because there are similarities.

Naming rules

URLs are named according to strict rules. We have already seen that email addresses and usenet newsgroups must conform to inter-nationally agreed formats.

Take the example above: http://www.ourschool.sch.uk

1. The *uk* shows that the web site is located in the United Kingdom.

2. The *sch* indicates that the web site is a school. Some schools use *ac* or *org*.

3. The *ourschool* is where the actual school name appears.

4. The *www* refers to the computer that handles the web traffic at the organisation's Internet Service Provider (ISP).

Taking care with web addresses

You need to remember that web addresses:

1. are case and punctuation sensitive
2. are usually in lower case, though they may contain capitals that must be typed
3. may contain the ~ (or **tilde)** character. (You can find this at the shifted hash key to the left of ENTER on your keyboard.)

Searching the web

What resources are available on the web?

In Chapter 1 we looked at the sorts of resources available on the internet. So what can teachers and schools expect to find on the web? Here is a brief summary:

▷ data files and publications

▷ online databases

▷ catalogues and guides to all kinds of libraries, art galleries and exhibitions

▷ maps, images from outer space, weather maps, millions of graphics images including clip art

▷ newspapers in English and all major foreign languages, entire books (especially classics)

▷ animations, multimedia presentations and video clips.

The list could go on almost indefinitely. But how do we find what we are looking for – especially when no one controls or indexes the web, and pages can come and go? Fortunately there are a number of search tools to overcome our problem.

What do we mean by search tools?

Search tools are remote programs that we can access in order to help us find relevant information. They can be on servers anywhere in the world. If you can access one nearer to home your searching will usually be faster.

Some search tools like **AltaVista** and **Lycos** are search engines and consist of databases of information that can be searched by using keywords or phrases. Others like **Yahoo!** are directories that have been indexed by human beings.

It is important to be aware of the differences between search engines and directories. They are often confused, so we will look at each category in turn.

Search engines

Search engines

These are also popularly called **spiders** or **crawlers**. Their search tools constantly visit web sites, creating ever more massive catalogues of web pages. Since they run automatically, and index millions of pages, these engines often find information not listed in directories. Their robot searchers have weird and wonderful names such as Scooter (AltaVista) and T-Rex (Lycos).

Directories

Directories are created by human beings, rather than electronically. Sites are submitted by the authors and assigned to appropriate categories. Because of the human input they can often provide better results than search engines. Yahoo! is the premier directory at present. It now has a UK section.

Hybrid search engines

To confuse matters further some search engines also have associated directories. The sites in the directory have usually been reviewed or rated. However, they are not usually trawled when a search takes place. You need to deliberately choose to see the reviews.

Note – the number of search programs available seems to vary on a daily basis. New ones burst forth on the market and older ones may die or buy out others. Hence we have restricted ourselves to the main programs which were current at the time of writing.

The major search engines

Where available, use their UK sites. They are usually quicker.

AltaVista
http://www.altavista.com
AltaVista opened in late 1995. It is now run by Compaq. It is recognised as a top program and partnered with **Yahoo!** as its preferred search engine until June 1998. It now uses a directory listing provided by **LookSmart** (see below).

Excite
http://www.excite.co.uk
http://www.excite.com
Launched 1995, Excite now has a UK presence. It has bought up **Magellan** and **WebCrawler**, both of which still operate independently. It also supports a directory format, divided into topics. Excite has recently offered 10 million email accounts to UK teachers and school students.

HotBot
http://www.hotbot.com
Launched in May 1996, HotBot is owned by *Wired*, the influential internet magazine. **Inktomi**, which emanates from UC Berkeley, provides the search engine.

Infoseek
http://www.infoseek.co.uk
http://www.infoseek.com
Launched in 1995, Infoseek is a well-received and well-connected search engine. It runs a separate directory.

Lycos
http://www.lycos.com
Lycos comes from the Latin for 'wolf-spider'. It originated 'way back' (!) in 1994. It has a separate directory. There is now a UK version at www.lycos.co.uk.

Microsoft
Microsoft was expected to launch its own search engine on MSN (the Microsoft Network) in mid-1998. Nothing has surfaced at the time of writing.

Northern Light
http://www.northernlight.com
Northern Light opened for business in the autumn of 1997. Northern Light is earnestly crawling large portions of the web. It could become an important program in the future. It has the ability to classify documents by topic but it does charge for specific search services. Perhaps this is a pointer to the future of searching on the internet.

WebCrawler
http://www.webcrawler.com
Launched in 1994 it is now owned by Excite. It has its own directory known as **WebCrawler Select**.

The major directories

Yahoo!
http://www.yahoo.co.uk
http://www.yahoo.com
Yahoo! is the major web site directory. It is well known, used and respected. Its directory covers 750,000 plus pages. Separate Yahoos! are available for countries and regions worldwide; for example, Yahoo! UK, Yahoo! France and Yahoo! Japan. There is even a Yahoo! for children called **Yahooligans!** (see below). Based on user submissions, it may not contain all the sites that a 'crawler' program might pick up. If Yahoo! doesn't turn up useful links you are automatically piped through to Inktomi. However, a host of major engines is offered to you at the foot of the page after a search.

LookSmart
http://www.looksmart.com
LookSmart is a human compiled directory with over 300,000 sites catalogued. It is found on Netscape's Net Search Page. Any searches that do not match its entries are sent to **AltaVista**.

Search programs

The main features of search programs (see Figure 38)

Size
These figures are only approximate. Some programs might have indexed pages more than once.

Pages crawled per day
The more pages crawled, the more likely that the index of the engine is up to date.

Date
This refers to whether the date that the file was created appears in the search program.

Submit time
This is how soon you can expect a page to appear in the search program index if it has been submitted by the author.

Boolean search
A Boolean search means one that uses 'operators' such as AND, OR and NOT. These can be used to narrow or widen the search. They can be very useful when thousands (or very few) hits have been received after the initial search.

Fig. 38. A summary of the main features of search programs.

Engine	AltaVista	Excite	HotBot	Infoseek	Lycos	Northern Light	Web-Crawler	Yahoo!
Size	Large	Large	Large	Medium	Medium	Medium	Small	–
Pages (in millions)	140	55	110	30	30	80	2	0.75
Pages crawled per day (in millions)	10	3	up to 10	–	6–10	3+	–	–
Date stamped?	Yes	No	File date	No	Yes	File date	No	–
Submit time	1 day	1–3 wks	1 day – 2 wks	Within 2 days	2–3 wks	2–4 wks	1–3 wks	
Boolean searches?	Yes	Yes	–	No	No	–	Yes	No
Case sensitive	Yes	No	Mixed	Yes	No	Mixed/title	No	No
Phrases	Yes	No	–	Yes	No	–	Yes	No
Results at a time (default)	10	10	10	10	5 10 15	25	25	No
Proximity	Yes (10)	No	–	Yes (100)	No	–	Yes	No
Results ranked	Yes	Yes	–	Yes	Yes	Yes	Yes	No
Wild cards	* after word	No	–	Yes	Yes	–	Yes	No
Directory	No	Yes	Yes	Yes	Yes	No	Yes	Yes!
Searches outside web	Usenet	Usenet	–	Usenet	FTP, Gopher	Special Collection	Usenet	No

Case sensitive
Search terms entered in lower case letters are case insensitive. The use of capital letters usually makes them case sensitive where the search engine supports this facility.

Phrases
The search engine can respond to questions phrased in everyday English.

Results at a time
This refers to how many results you can display at a time. The default number(s) is shown.

Proximity
This causes a hit if the search term(s) are found within a certain number of words of each other. Engines will often search for a term varying from anything from 1 to 100 words distance from each other.

Results ranked
Many search tools will rank results in some way. Usually the higher the match between the page and the search term, the greater the ranking assigned to the result.

Wild cards
With simple queries you can add a wild card character at the beginning or end of phrases or words. These will stand for any letter or combination of letters. Many allow the use of a * (star). For example hess* will find hesse, hessen and hessian.

Directory
The search tool offers a hierarchically arranged subject index similar to Yahoo!

Searches outside the web
Services searched might include usenet, gopher or FTP.

Search engines versus directories

So should you use a search engine or a directory? The advantages and disadvantages of each are summarised in the table overleaf. You can of course use both, or as many as you like.

As well as search engines and directories, there are other search programs you can investigate.

Meta tools

These are search programs that combine several engines. They are fast but do not have the sophistication of the individual programs.

Specialised searching ....

Search engines	Directories
Useful for specific information.	Useful for general information.
Not censored or sifted. Information not evaluated – so an amount of inappropriate material is often found after a search.	Information evaluated and censorship undertaken. House style might exclude some material.
Robots can only find web pages that are linked to other pages.	Compiled by humans. Site authors submit their own pages.
No search engine can cover the entire net.	
Have larger databases than directories.	

Ask Jeeves
http://www.askjeeves.com
Ask Jeeves allows you to type in questions in standard English. If it cannot find a match within its own data it will show results from other engines.

Savvy Search
www.savvysearch.com

Specialised search engines

Bigfoot
http://www.bigfoot.co.uk
As we have seen, Bigfoot is worth trying for email addresses.

Dejanews
http://www.dejanews.com
The most popular usenet search facility.

Four11
http://www.four11.com
For US addresses you could also try Four11.

Internet Yellow Pages
http://www.yell.co.uk.
Particularly good for travel and entertainment information.

Supernews
http://www.supernews.com
Another means of searching for usenet postings.

Search engines for school students

Over the past year several search engines have been developed for family and student use. These aim to avoid producing unpleasant images and materials amongst their 'hits'.

Ask Jeeves for Kids

http://www.ajkids.com
Like the adult version it can take straightforward questions.

Disney Internet Guide

http://www.disney.com/dig/today
This only displays sites thought suitable for children.

Kids Search Tools

http://www.rcls.org/ksearch.htm
This site brings together a variety of search tools suitable for school children.

Lycos SafetyNet

http://personal.lycos.com/safetynet/safetynet.asp
This allows parents to block out unsuitable sites from Lycos search results.

Yahooligans!

http://www.yahooligans.com
Aimed at 7 to 12-year-olds. It contains handpicked sites and does not feature advertising aimed at adults.

Fig. 39. Walt Disney's DIG site has a US bias, but includes a useful Homework Help section.

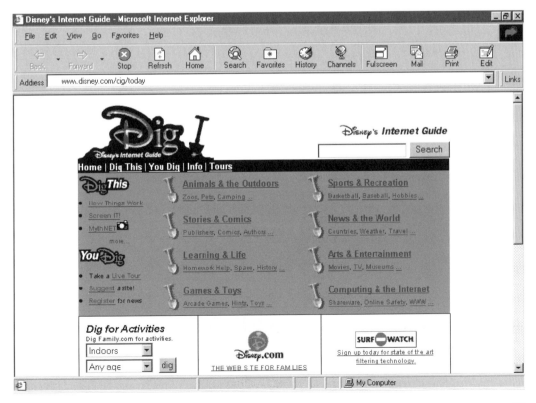

Tips for searching......................................

Fig. 40. Ask Jeeves
for Kids.

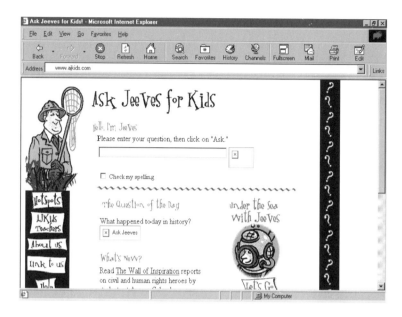

Tips for searching

The following tips will help whatever program you use.

1. For general information use Yahoo! For specific information use AltaVista, Excite etc.

2. Encasing a term or phrase in quotation marks narrows down your search considerably, because only that combination of words (**string**) will be found.

3. Try several programs – Yahoo! is useful here in that it allows you to connect to a variety of engines easily.

4. The same keyword may have very different levels of success in a range of engines.

5. Experiment with wild cards. Most engines will accept a * (which stands for any number of characters) and ? (which stands for one character). AltaVista accepts + and - as filters. Always read the help pages that come with engines like AltaVista and Northern Light. They are often excellent. Print them out!

6. Boolean operators (expressions like AND, OR and NOT) allow you to be more specific in your search. They are accepted by many search engines. Some engines allow you to use extra operators such as ADJACENT, NEAR and FOLLOWED BY. Experiment with these, but be aware that you might restrict your search so much that you end up with no result after a search.

7. **Bookmark** your search result if you think you might want to use it again (see Figure 42 showing how to save your favourite sites).

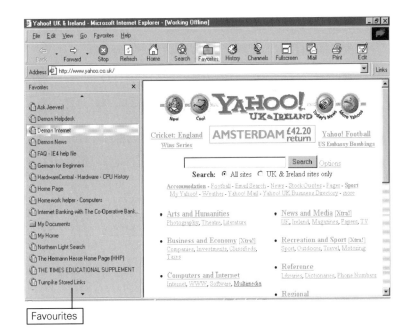

Fig. 41. 'Favorites' list in Internet Explorer. In *Netscape* favorites are known as **bookmarks**.

Favourites

General tips for using the web

▷ Use the web in the morning or late evening, it's usually faster (the USA is not online).

▷ Use UK mirror sites, especially when downloading data or programs.

▷ Set the home page in your browser to open up with a UK site, for example Yahoo!'s UK site at http://www.yahoo.co.uk. The default page in Internet Explorer is often the US Microsoft site. See Fig. 43.

▷ Investigate purchasing a copy of Secret Agent or Unmozify to read your local cache. However, Internet Explorer 5 has improved cache reading facilities.

▷ Your ISP might cache its most frequently visited web pages. They will advise you how to alter the settings on your browser in order to take advantage of this.

Fig. 42. Adding Yahoo! UK to the favourites list.

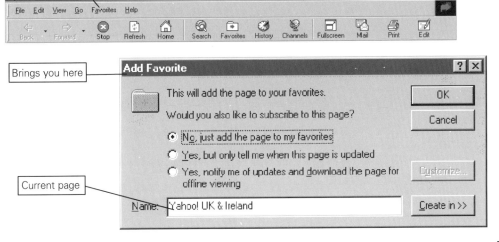

Fig. 43. Setting your home page in Internet Explorer to Yahoo!'s UK site. Follow the route in your browser: View▶Options▶General.

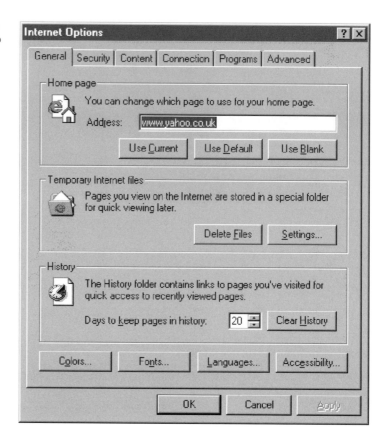

▷ If transfer is interrupted or transfer speeds are slow, hit the Reload/Refresh button in your browser.

Example: a step-by-step guide to searching for information in AltaVista

The following screen shots (Figures 44–49) show you how to search for something really useful – an OFSTED report! You are shown a *simple search*; this is a search without ANDs, ORs or NOTs.

Fig. 44. AltaVista's initial search page.

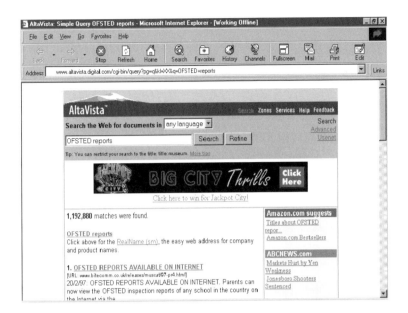

Fig. 45. Search for OFSTED reports brings up over a million 'hits'!

This looks a good site to try out first (mentions OFSTED by name in main part of URL)

Fig. 46. Some of the results of the search for OFSTED Reports.

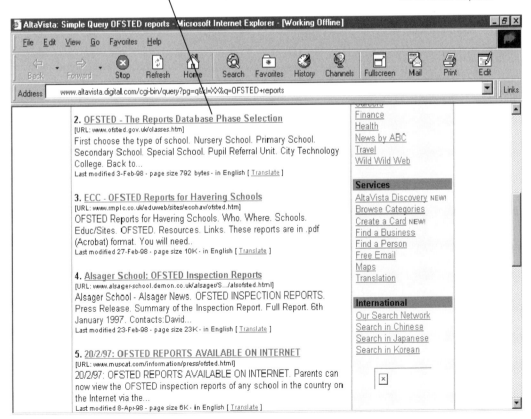

Fig. 47. Choose phase of school.

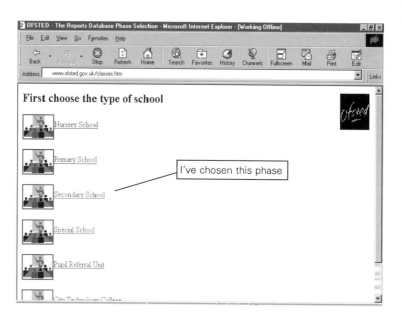

Fig. 48. Choose your LEA.

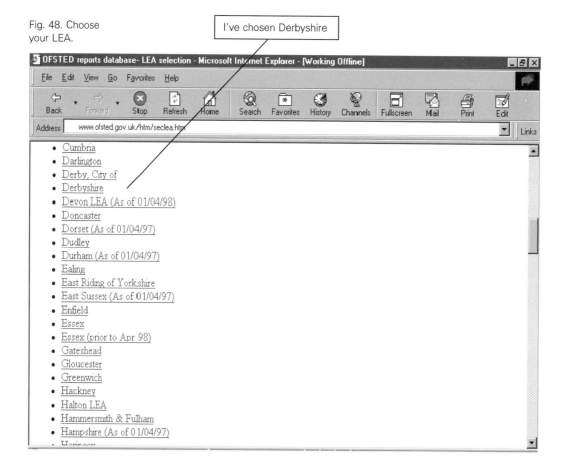

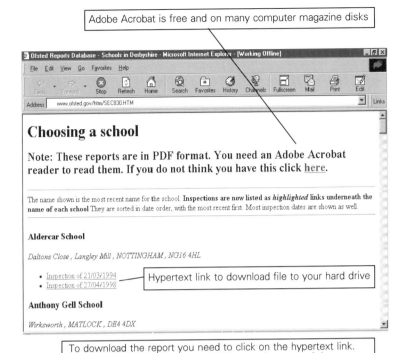

Adobe Acrobat is free and on many computer magazine disks

Fig. 49. Choose your school.

Choosing a school

Note: These reports are in PDF format. You need an Adobe Acrobat reader to read them. If you do not think you have this click here.

The name shown is the most recent name for the school. **Inspections are now listed as** *highlighted* **links underneath the name of each school** They are sorted in date order, with the most recent first. Most inspection dates are shown as well.

Aldercar School

Daltons Close, Langley Mill, NOTTINGHAM, NG16 4HL

- Inspection of 21/03/1994
- Inspection of 27/04/1998

Hypertext link to download file to your hard drive

Anthony Gell School

Wirksworth, MATLOCK, DE4 4DX

To download the report you need to click on the hypertext link. You will need a program called Adobe Acrobat to read the reports. It is widely available from computer magazine disks

Project

An excellent project for teachers would be to produce a short guide for students with web references. This could take the form of a web page (refer to later chapters on web page construction and **intranets**), or just a word-processed handout.

You could cover the following:

▷ a topic from an examination syllabus

▷ extension work for students who have completed core activities

▷ a project that needed to use up-to-date data from the internet especially in subjects such as Business Studies, Geography and IT.

Questions and answers

What is a 'plug-in'?
It is a program that adds extra features to a browser. For example, allows it to play video clips and sound files. The most popular plug-in is **RealPlayer.** It allows you to play live audio, radio and video across the internet (see Appendix for address).

How did the web start?
The web originated with UK scientist Tim Berners-Lee at CERN (the

Questions and answers

European Laboratory for Particle Physics) in the 1980s. At its heart was a programming language called HTML (hypertext mark-up language). In the early days it was used for displaying text-based research papers.

What is meant by cache?
In relation to the internet, cache refers to a directory on your hard-drive or network drive. Into this directory your browser program stores the pages it downloads from the web. It is possible to view these pages offline (not connected to the web) through your browser.

How can you read cache?
It is easy enough to use Internet Explorer or Netscape offline to read your web page cache. However, there are specialised programs to do this, which are more versatile. **Secret Agent** is one such shareware, and it is very easy to use. We rate it as one of the most useful programs to use with the web.

What is a mirror site?
This is a web site with a copy of the files found on another site. Mirrors are available of US sites in Europe. Accessing the nearest site obviously saves you money in telephone bills. The well-known

Fig. 50. Secret Agent's cache reading program.

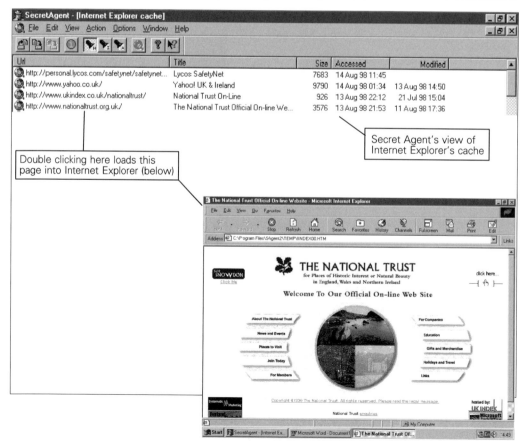

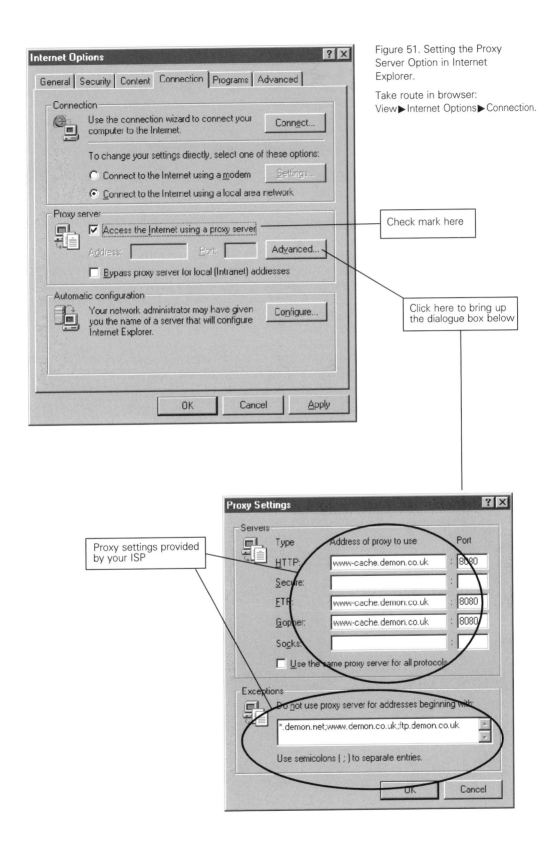

Figure 51. Setting the Proxy
Server Option in Internet
Explorer.

Take route in browser:
View▶Internet Options▶Connection.

Check mark here

Click here to bring up
the dialogue box below

Proxy settings provided
by your ISP

Proxy servers..

Tucows shareware site has several mirrors throughout the world and is a good site for downloading a range of internet tools. It has a UK mirror on the CIX site. (See Appendix.)

What is a proxy server?
This is a computer usually provided by your internet provider which holds the most used pages by its subscribers. Setting your browser to access this proxy service should, in theory, speed up your internet access especially if you often access popular sites.

Summary

Fig. 52. The home page of the Tucows web site, showing 'mirror' sites all over the world.

In this chapter we have looked at the web, how it is organised, how to trawl through it and how to make the best use of it. The web, however, is a globally vast and chaotic place and is the depository of a lot of material unsuitable for young people. In the next chapter we will be examining issues of filtering web content and strategies that can be employed to ensure that web access is handled sensibly.

7 Play safe on the internet

In this chapter you will be introduced to the following topics:

▶ *web access issues*
▶ *restricting access to unsuitable materials*
▶ *how filtering software works*
▶ *dealing with pornography*
▶ *rules for online safety*
▶ *acceptable use policies and contracts.*

. . . .

The educational value of online systems and the wealth of useful material greatly outweigh the risks, but there are risks. These include the delivery of hate mail, and the availability of racist material, pornography, and violent and inflammatory publications.

All teachers act *in loco parentis* to their students. It is the teachers' responsibility to ensure that their students are taught how to use the internet sensibly and also minimise their access to unsuitable material.

The problem of suppressing inappropriate material is something that is not new or unique to the web or to the wider internet. We recognise that there is plenty of unsuitable material in magazines, newspapers, videos, and television programmes available through satellite and cable systems. As responsible adults we realise that students need to be shielded from this material.

The problem with the internet is that the material is by its nature intangible. Nor is it restricted to one site. There is an additional problem in that most parents and teachers do not really understand this medium and many students are well in advance of their elders in the ability to access the internet.

A balancing act

Allowing access to the internet in schools basically means a balancing act between freedom to roam and some restrictions on movement. But just because the determined 14-year-old will find his/her way around restrictions does not mean that no limitations at all should be put into place.

How do we restrict access to unsuitable materials?

Web filtering systems are available but these are not a substitute for teaching responsible use of the internet. Filtering software can be installed on the network server (server-side filtering) or on the individual machine (client-side filtering).

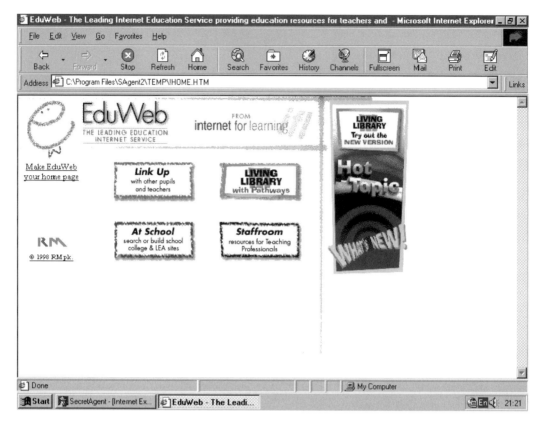

Fig. 53. Research
Machines provides a
'walled garden'
environment for schools
through its Internet for
Learning offshoot.

Server-side filtering

This is where the filtering software is installed on the server. This
software can be on the local server on the school network, or it can be
on the server of your ISP. This system is safer because it cannot be
easily tampered with by determined students.

Server-side filtering is used to produce what are known as **walled
environments**. Web access is filtered by blocking out unsuitable sites.
Extra services are provided such as discussion groups and indexed
curriculum material. The banned sites list is updated on a regular basis.
This is not foolproof as sites can change their location and name on a
daily basis, and the effectiveness depends on the vigilance of teachers
and the ISP filtering team.

Companies providing such facilities include:

▷ Research Machines (Internet for Learning)
▷ BT Campus World
▷ Edex.

Client-side filtering

This software is installed on each individual machine. Obviously, in a
school without a network, or one restricted to a single machine on the
internet, this is your only option. On single machines, AOL's service
gives the teacher account-holder quite a lot of control over what access
the students have to the internet.

How filtering software works

There are three main ways of filtering web access.

1. Blocking out access to unsuitable URLs. This can be very time-consuming to the individual and is best left to an internet provider. It is possible for schools to set up their own proxy servers and use them to restrict access to sites.

2. Checking text on web pages for unsuitable words and phrases. This can have unfortunate and unpredictable results. For example, it may deny you access to sites on Middlesex! (**Net Nanny** is one of many such products to aid parents and teachers restrict access to unpleasant material. See the Appendix and Questions and Answers below.)

3. Preventing the download of executable files (programs) or graphics.

Dealing with pornography

The parents' role

Parents need to learn and use the internet alongside their children. They need to give their children guidance according to their values, just as they give advice about the watching of radio and television programmes. There are several good information sources:

▷ Excellent leaflets are available from BECTA (the former National Council of Educational Technology).

▷ There are many web sites that deal with child safety on the internet.

▷ Yahoo! has an excellent series of advice pages in its **Yahooligans!** section. Larry Magid has also provided an excellent page of advice. His rules for online safety are summarised below (page 84).

The teachers' role

Teachers also have a responsibility here. They need to be aware of the nature of materials available. They must be able to recognise when students are not where they should be!

Every school needs to have **acceptable use policies** for everyone using its IT systems and the internet. Plenty of these can be found through any web search engine. Some samples are shown below.

IT staff can run a Parents' Evening to explain to parents the school policies and systems, as well as outlining the sorts of strategies that they could employ at home with their sons and daughters.

Shielding systems . . . .

IT staff need to:

▷ consider the location of the machines (a good line of sight is needed for the supervisor)

▷ use auditing software which tracks the sites visited by students

▷ monitor the use of printing facilities. A sensible solution is to arrange for central printing for materials produced outside supervised lesson time.

A number of other solutions can also be considered.

Shielding systems

Some sites now ask for a statement of age before entry. This is obviously easy to circumvent. Increasingly, sites that contain controversial material ask for a password that is issued on the production of a credit card or other identifying material. This is not perfect, but at least a start has been made.

Site ratings

Fig. 54. Accessing 'Content Advisor' through the Internet Explorer browser.

In this solution site owners agree to tag their pages according to a rating system similar to that used in the video recording industry.

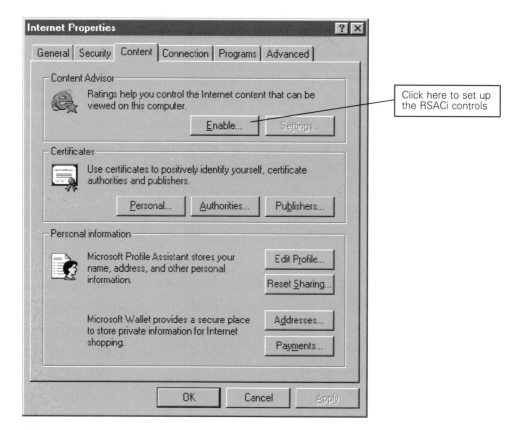

Recreational Software Advisory Council

One of the main bodies providing a rating system is the Recreational Software Advisory Council. This is an independent non-profit organisation based in Washington DC, USA. It has developed the RSACi system that ranks material according to varying levels of sex, nudity, violence and offensive language on web sites and in computer games.

Site owners grade their pages through filling in an online form on the RSAC site. RSAC then issues them with some special HTML code that is then placed at the top of their web pages. Teachers and parents can then set the levels allowed to their youngsters within the web browser program. In Internet Explorer this can be set through the route:

Control Panel ▶ Internet ▶ Content ▶ Content Advisor

The settings are password-protected by the adult in charge of the browsing software. A common format that allows rating systems to be read by browsers is being developed by PICS (Platform for Internet Content Selection) at the Massachusetts Institute of Technology.

It is hoped that self-regulation will prevent national governments censoring the internet (see below).

Fig. 55. Setting the RSACi ratings for use of language in Internet Explorer.

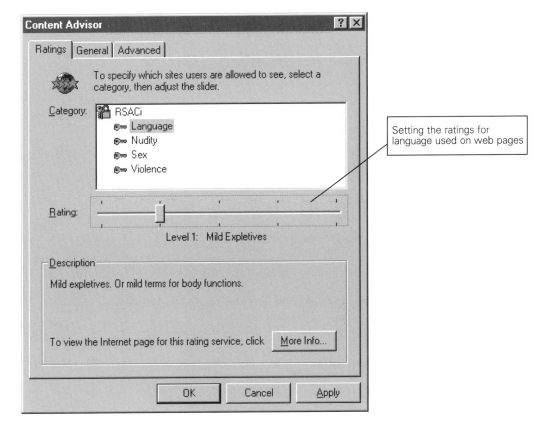

Setting the ratings for language used on web pages

83

Online safety ....

Rating by a third party

Here, an outside body trawls the internet to visit sites and then rates them according to the system described above. This could take up a lot of time for the rating body since hundreds of thousands of new sites appear each month. Furthermore, agreeing to what type of material deserved a particular rating could exhaust many thousands of hours of debate.

Online safety

The following rules for safe use of the internet are adapted from the work of Lawrence J. Magid. This can be found on the site of the National Center for Missing and Exploited Children (see Appendix). Similar materials can be found on the Smartparent site. These materials form a good discussion point with students. They can be printed on card and placed in student diaries or organisers for reference.

My Rules for Online Safety

1. I will not give out personal information such as my address, telephone number, parents' work address/telephone number, or the name and location of my school without my parents' permission.

2. I will tell my parents right away if I come across any information that makes me feel uncomfortable.

3. I will never agree to get together with someone I 'meet' online without first checking with my parents. If my parents agree to the meeting, I will be sure that it is in a public place and bring my mother or father along.

4. I will never send a person my picture or anything else without first checking with my parents.

5. I will not respond to any messages that in any way make me feel uncomfortable. It is not my fault if I get a message like that. If I do I will tell my parents right away so that they can contact the online service.

6. I will talk with my parents so that we can set up rules for going online. We will decide upon the time of day that I can be online, the length of time I can be online, and appropriate areas for me to visit. I will not access other areas or break these rules without their permission.

School web sites

On school web sites students' photographs, names, addresses and telephone numbers should not be included unless there are exceptional reasons.

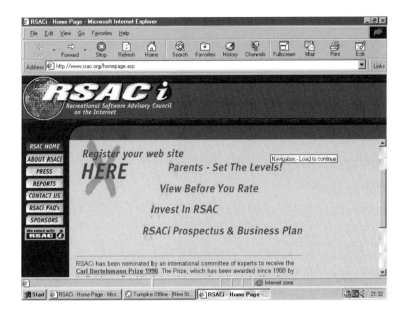

Fig. 56. The RSACi Home Page. You can register your site here and learn more about the ratings system. The initials stand for Recreational Software Advisory Council on the Internet.

Acceptable use policies

All schools need to produce policies for the acceptable use of IT facilities and student guidelines to complement these policies. The specimen contract below is an amalgam of several others produced by institutions in the USA and the UK.

Internet Contract

Student first name: _____   Last name: _____

1. I agree to use the internet sensibly and take note of the following conditions:

2. I will not deliberately search for material that is inappropriate to my studies or schoolwork generally.

3. I will not participate in chat rooms without permission of my tutors.

4. I will not send offensive or inappropriate email to other users and will observe the rules of etiquette in email and newsgroups that I have access to.

5. I will not download images, programs, and any files without permission into any user area on the College network system.

6. Any inappropriate use of the internet will lead to permanent exclusion from internet access.

7. I have discussed my use of the internet with my parents.

Student's signature: _____

Tutor group: _____

Date: _____

Parent's signature: _____

Suggested guidelines ....

Guidelines

Alongside the contract, students and parents need to be provided with a set of guidelines. These might take the following format:

General comments

▷ Here there might be reference to **netiquette**. The comments could refer to the fact that student areas can be scanned periodically. There could be a reminder that email is not secure and can be read by others (in other words, teachers and technicians). Basic rules about bringing disks to school and transferring data to student areas should be covered here also (no illegal software or inappropriate material).

What is not permitted

▷ Include here a warning about misuse of email (such as bullying), infringements of copyright (software and web resources), use of bad language, and time-wasting on the system.

Sanctions

▷ These might vary from removal from the IT system for a short period of time to notification to the governors or police if necessary.

Projects

▷ Produce an Acceptable Use Policy for your school. Visit Web66 and the ACITT sites to view some current policies.

▷ Produce a set of guidelines to be inserted into student organisers/ diaries.

Questions and answers

What filtering programs are available for home use?
The main programs available are **NetNanny**, **Cybersitter**, **Cyber Patrol** and **Surf Watch**. All of these can be trialled and are often found on magazine disks.

What filtering programs are available for use in schools?
Other than using a filtered service, schools could investigate setting up their own proxy server (see Chapter 6) and also investigate the program called **Wingate Pro**. Otherwise you could try the following programs: **Watchdog**, **Cybertimer** and **Time's Up**.

What programs are available to keep track of where students have surfed and how can we restrict their access by time?
Until recently there was practically nothing available, but now a product called Webranger is available for evaluation at www.rangersuite.com. This product could be very useful to school IT managers.

Summary

In this chapter we have looked at the issues concerned with safe access of the internet in schools and how teachers and parents can help protect their students and offspring from accessing unpleasant material on the internet.

In the next chapter we will look at writing a simple home page for a teacher or a small department.

Fig. 57. Surfwatch for filtering.

8 Writing your first home page

This chapter will introduce you to:

▶ *what characteristics make up a good home page*
▶ *how to design your home page*
▶ *how to build your home page*
▶ *how to put your page online.*

. . . .

What is a home page?

Most pages on the world wide web are home pages. Designed by the general public, home pages contain information on literally any topic that you can think of. They are characteristically small in size, consisting of very few pages in total (often just one). Consequently it takes only a little knowledge and commitment, in terms of time, to make that transition from a passive recipient of information (a user) to becoming an active publisher.

This presents teachers with several opportunities:

▷ good ideas and practice can be shared with other fellow teachers locally and all over the world

▷ resources can be accessed in real-time and used straight away

▷ such pages can act as a forum for discussion and problem-solving.

What characteristics make up a good home page?

Regardless of how much you may read about successful design techniques, the best way of finding out the qualities of a good web page is still to go online and see for yourself. It would be a great idea to take some time now to access the web, find a search engine and key in 'home page' as your search criteria. Take a little time to browse the pages that come up, making some notes about what makes these pages stand out. Note what factors make some pages irritating, too. This experience will be invaluable when you come to author your own page later on.

Finally, let us look at some examples to make things clear about how the content you choose to include influences the design.

Case studies

Jim keeps things simple

Jim teaches Geography in a secondary comprehensive. He has written his home page to act as a resource for other professionals like him. It is clearly laid out, with easily followed links and relevant content. Another positive point is that it is really fast for people to download because he has kept the number of images to a bare minimum.

Phil is more 'flashy'

Phil is a primary school teacher and wants a more visually attractive page for use by younger students. He has therefore incorporated several scanned photos and clip art images into the page, along with a snazzy theme. The idea is to ensure the youngsters do not get bored. Unfortunately this made the page bigger (in terms of file size), meaning that it took rather longer for people to access.

Questions and answers

What factors go to make up a really impressive home page?
We could summarise them like this:

▷ relevant content for the targeted users

▷ a minimal access time, so that downloading doesn't take forever

▷ explicit and obvious internal links which make navigation around the page easy

▷ accurate and up-to-date hyperlinks to other related sites

▷ a consistent and appropriate design theme throughout.

Designing your own home page

Now that you have some idea about the characteristics of a good home page, it is time to begin the project of building your own. Obviously some focused thought in the design stages will make the page that much more successful.

Where to start

In this section we will assume that you will be designing a web page containing just a single page. Once your project increases to more than just one page it can be considered a 'site'. We will go into site design and construction in more detail later.

Back to that initial project first, though. So where do you begin? Spend five or ten minutes with a blank sheet of paper, a pen and ask yourself the following two questions to get your page on track.

1.   Who do I want my page to be aimed at?
In Jim's example above it is other Secondary Geography teachers like himself. With Phil his audience was wider, which had implications for the style and content.

2.   What content would the target audience find useful?
Jim wants to include some teaching resources he developed to help

Writing the page ....

integrate IT into Key Stage 3 Geography. Phil, on the other hand, is concentrating on telling colleagues about his curriculum maps for Key Stage 3, and some quizzes and project ideas for the students to use.

Remembering to keep the design simple at this stage, sketch what you think the page should look like. Figure 58 (below) shows Jim's initial ideas.

Hopefully you now have a pretty good idea what your home page will contain, so the next logical step is to actually write it. What you will be doing shortly is

(a) creating your page on the computer hard disk

(b) testing it to see whether it works

(c) then actually putting your page onto the web.

How do I write the page?

There are many software applications today which save you having to type in the HTML code to construct a web page. Usually they allow you to work in a WYSIWYG (What You See Is What You Get) environment, much like a desktop-publishing application. The software automatically converts what you have created into the necessary HTML.

Fig. 58. Jim's initial ideas for his home page.

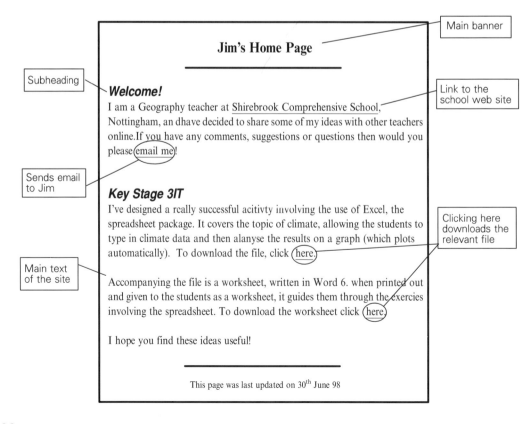

90

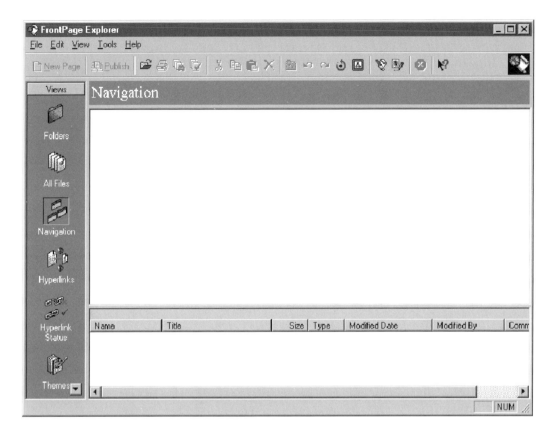

Fig. 59. The FrontPage
Explorer start-up screen.

▷ We will assume that you are going to be using Microsoft
FrontPage to create your masterpiece. This package is very
popular, relatively inexpensive (about £100), and a purpose-built
piece of software which is quite easy to use. One drawback is that
not every internet service provider has the necessary 'Microsoft
FrontPage Extensions' required for you to take advantage of some
of the more advanced features the software offers. Check that
your own ISP does.

▷ If you are on a really tight budget, go for a non-specialist page
creator like the extra tools in Microsoft Word in the Office 97 suite;
here you can convert your documents to web pages with a click of
the mouse.

▷ If you have Netscape Communicator (4.0 or later) as your browser,
you will find it includes 'Page Composer'. This makes it very easy
to author simple web pages. You can add lots of hyperlinks, colour
backgrounds, images and tables. You can download it free from
the internet, and often find it on magazine disks (currently version
4.5).

The first stage is to install the software to your system. As you are
running Windows 95 or 98 this is really easy to do; in fact quite often all
you have to do is insert the CD-ROM, be persistent and keep on
clicking the 'next' prompt buttons until your screen gives you a
message such as 'Installation sucessfully completed'.

Using FrontPage ....

How do I create just a single blank page?
When you are all installed, you will be presented with a screen that looks very much like the one in Figure 59 (page 91).

Set the ball rolling by telling the software that you want just a single blank page. This is achieved by using the mouse to click File/New Page. A dialogue box will appear, which hopefully resembles closely the example in Figure 60. Ensure that the 'One-Page Web' radio button is selected. Let us keep it simple first time around!

Next you are going to give your page a title. To do this, click in the white text box and get rid of that annoying default name ('My New Web'). Then click on OK.

FrontPage will now open up what is called the FrontPage Explorer. More on this later. All you need to do now is a little customisation and content adding, and that page is complete.

Fig. 60. New FrontPage web dialogue box.

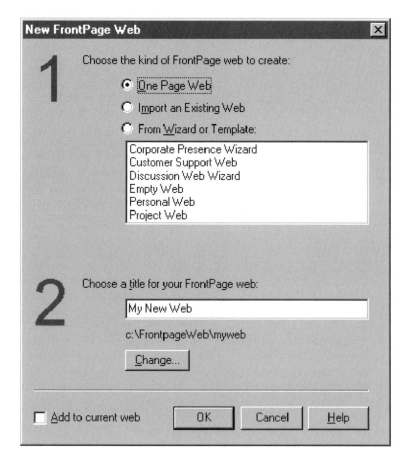

How FrontPage works

First of all, though, you will need to know a little about how FrontPage works. A small investment in time here will enable you to reap rewards later on. Don't worry, it is really very easy to get to grips with!

FrontPage consists of two main areas within which you will be working. These are known as:

▷ FrontPage Explorer

▷ FrontPage Editor.

Here's what each part of the program is used for:

FrontPage Explorer

This feature of FrontPage is used to manage the whole of your web site, carrying out procedures such as adding new pages, deleting pages you do not want any more and generally keeping track of all the files contained within your site.

FrontPage Editor

The FrontPage Editor is used to add content to the pages. It works much like a DTP (desktop publishing) package. Of course there are

Fig. 61. Changing views in FrontPage Explorer.

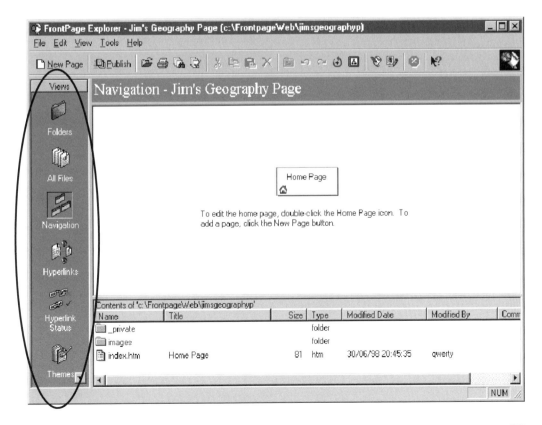

Adding a theme to your home page........................

many extra features included. These allow you to do things such as include hyperlinks to other pages, or create some amazing effects using ActiveX controls.

FrontPage Explorer – changing 'views'

FrontPage Explorer allows you to view your site in many different ways. Different views are selected using the button bar on the left of the screen, as circled in Figure 61 (page 93). As you can see in the diagram, 'Navigation' view is selected. This is where you need to start. In Navigation view a box represents each page of your site. The lines between them are hyperlinks. Because the site above only contains one page, there is only one box.

To begin the next task in the project, you will need to open up the FrontPage Editor. You will actually start editing your page towards the design you sketched out earlier. This will involve opening your page in the FrontPage Editor.

How do I add a theme to my home page?
'Theme' is the term used to describe the overall style of a page, including the colour schemes, font colours, sizes and so on. So how do you decide on one? Easy.

The first thing is to open the FrontPage Editor. Double click on the page to open. In this example your choice is limited to one. You should see the Editor open into a window like the one below.

Fig. 62. Adding a theme to your web page.

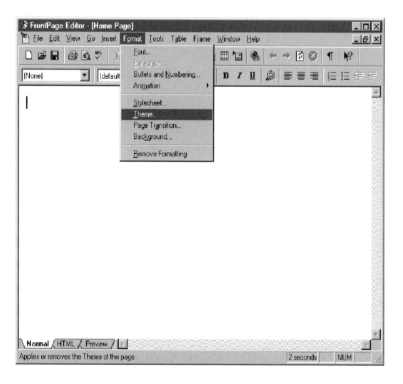

As in Figure 62, go to Format/Theme. You will be presented with a large selection of pre-designed themes to choose from. You can browse them all by just clicking once on each. Jim decided to choose the theme called Expedition, as it seemed to have the right feel for a geography page!

Click OK to add that theme to your home page. Now it is time to start typing in the actual content.

How do I add content?
The Editor acts just like many popular DTP applications. It should present few problems when it comes to keying-in the text that you want. We recommend you use the 'styles' defined for each theme. You can use the styles to format your text into headings, sub-headings and main text.

To select a style, simply click on the drop-down list and choose from the selection available, as shown in Figure 63.

Spend some time typing in the text of your page, not forgetting to keep saving!

You should finally end up with something like Jim's page, shown in Figure 64.

Fig. 63. Choosing and using styles.

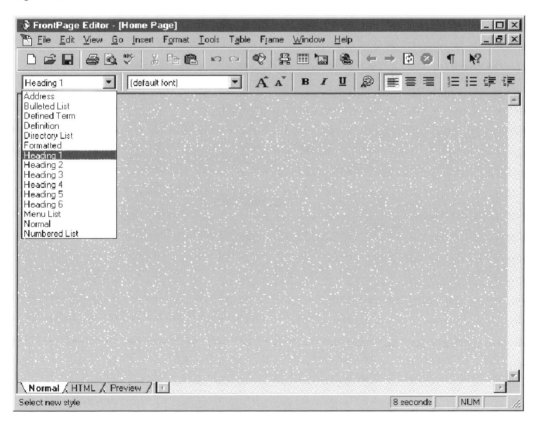

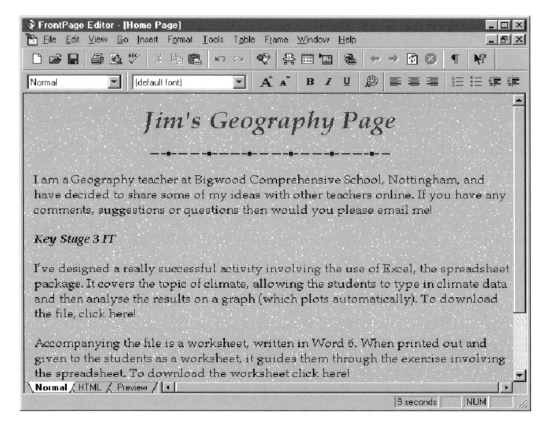

Fig. 64. Jim's finished web page.

Remember those hyperlinks that Jim put into his page in the design stages? Well, they activated an email to Jim and two file downloads. They are really easy to set up, too.

How do I set up a hyperlink?
First select the text that you want to form the hyperlink. Next go to Insert/Hyperlink, as in Figure 65.

Fig. 65. Setting up a hyperlink.

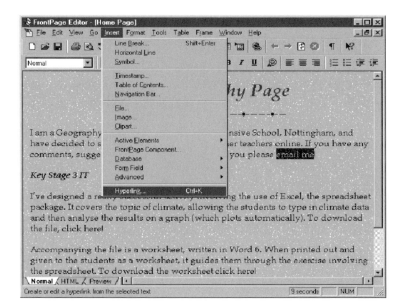

When the hyperlink dialogue box pops up, you have got some choices to make. What exactly do you want to link to? In the example, Jim wants a hyperlink to his email address, so he selects the envelope button (circled in Figure 66).

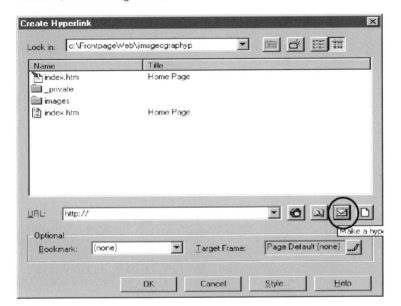

Fig. 66. Making a 'mailto:' hyperlink.

Up pops yet another dialogue box (Figure 67).

Finally he will type in his email address as in the example. Hit 'return' a couple of times and your hyperlink is in place.

Carry out the same procedure for the other hyperlinks in your page, but instead of doing an email, select the other buttons available, creating a link to a file on your computer or another page on the web.

How do I put the page online?
With FrontPage it is really easy. First, save your page in the Editor and return to the FrontPage Explorer. Then connect to your Internet Provider as usual. Finally, simply click on the 'Publish' button. FrontPage will then transfer all of the files to your Internet Provider. Your page should now be online!

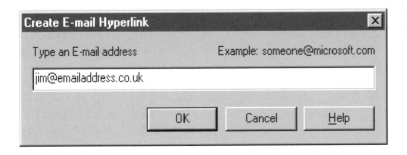

Fig. 67. Adding the email address to hyperlink to.

Summary ....

If you used a software package such as Microsoft Publisher or Word 97 to produce your page, then getting it online will be a little more difficult. More on that in Chapter 10.

Summary

In this chapter we have looked at what a home page is on the world wide web. We have also identified the characteristics that go to make up a good home page along with how to design and build one using generic software.

In the next chapter we will look at how to design and build a more elaborate web site for a school, consisting of several linked pages.

Examples of school web sites. *Right* the home page of an Australian school, and *below* the home page of an English school in Spain.

9 Producing a school web site

In this chapter you will find out how to:

▶ *design a school web site with useful content*
▶ *build the web site and make it attractive to use*
▶ *manage the site, ensuring it is kept up to date.*

. . . .

Designing a school web site

Deciding on the content

Isn't a school web site just a larger version of a web page?
The answer is simply 'no'. Just as different kinds of newspapers are tailored towards different markets, web pages too are written to fulfil a variety of functions.

The simple web page that we discussed in the previous chapter could be thought of as a relatively simple newsletter – concise, to the point and reflecting your own personal style. The main difference between a web *site* and a web *page* is scale. A site consists of several or many individual pages, linked together to form a whole suite of information. The second difference is obviously content, and it is worth thinking about that a little more.

What kind of image do you want to portray?

Just as with a school magazine, you need to think very carefully about the type of image you want your web site to convey.

▷ *Remember* – individuals can view these pages from potentially anywhere in the world. They will form an opinion of the school based on your efforts!

Once again, a great starting point is to see what is already out there and see what impressions you get from the sites online. Yahoo! makes a good starting point, so use the categories available to find school sites. When browsing, make notes of features that you find appealing or particularly useful. In contrast, jot down annoying features too, so that you will remember what to avoid.

The prospectus approach

In general you will find that most school web sites look just like a prospectus. The vast majority place their school logo or a photograph on the main title (or index) page, with clear links to other sub-topics from there.

Case study ....

These sub-topics or pages typically include sections containing:

1. a mission statement

2. a tour of the site

3. links to sites of local interest

4. students' work

5. curriculum details

6. contact information.

Having seen some school web sites you will soon get a feel about what you want to include in your own site. Again, planning is the key. Get out pen and paper and draw a flow-diagram to show all the sections you want to include, and how they relate to each other. Each box in the flow diagram can represent a page; the lines between the boxes can represent hyperlinks.

Case study

Jim is not too ambitious at first

As this was really a personal project, Jim decided that his school's web site should not be too ambitious. He therefore kept things relatively simple. This should make it much less time-consuming to get the site up and running. He could always add to it later.

Figure 68 shows Jim's sketch for the site structure. So, for example, when someone accesses the site, the first page they see is the 'Welcome Page'. From here there are links to two other pages, one called 'Curriculum Areas' and one called 'Contact Information'. From each of these there are links, too.

Fig. 68. Jim's site plan.

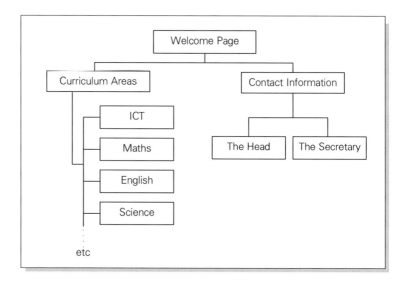

Where will I get the content?

Although Jim's web site design seems very simple, it is actually quite an ambitious project. Remember that writing the pages should not be too much of a headache for Jim as he has already written his own home page. What could prove difficult is collecting the material from the different curriculum areas.

Always bear this in mind when designing a site, and ask yourself the question above. You do not want the project held up just because you are not getting the content from a particular department. Be prepared to be flexible. Do not worry if your site does not start with the full complement of subjects. What matters most is to get it up and running. Adding more pages later is no problem.

Building the site

Having browsed some of the available content you may have noticed a particular feature of many web sites out there. Some pages seem to have divided up the screen into two or three sections, as in the diagram below. This makes the site not only more attractive, but also much easier to get around. This is a feature called **frames**, where each section of the web page always has a different content. Figure 69 demonstrates a typical page layout using frames.

Frame 1
Contains a banner which contains the title, displaying what the main content of the page is about.

Frame 2
Contains the navigation buttons that allow the user to browse between pages through the site. This frame usually remains the same.

Frame 3
Holds the main content of the page, relating to the navigation button that has been selected in frame 2.

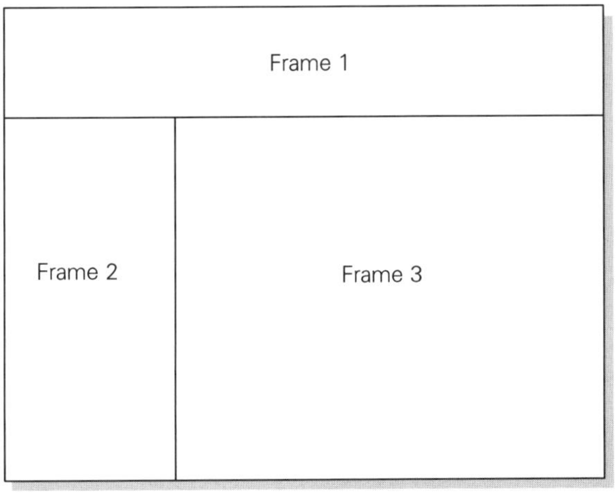

Fig. 69. A typical page layout using frames.

Using frames ....

How can I take advantage of frames?

Fortunately Microsoft FrontPage has built-in features that do most of the work for you. You can take full advantage of using frames whilst doing little of the work. In short, you get to take the credit for a really slick web site!

You start out as before, by loading the FrontPage Explorer. Then select File/New/FrontPage Web, as in Figure 70.

A dialogue box should open up which asks you what type of web site you want to open, as illustrated in Figure 71. Included in there is a list of pre-designed templates that FrontPage has on offer.

Select the one called 'Personal Web'. Then, in the text box below, type in the name of your school. The software will now set up a template for your site containing four linked pages called 'Homepage', 'Interests', 'Photo Album' and 'Favourites'. No doubt you will want to change these names, which we will do later.

How do I apply a theme to a whole site?

Fig. 70. Beginning to create a page with frames.

Again the software makes what could be a difficult task very easy. From the FrontPage Explorer, find the button on the left labelled 'Themes'. When pressed, you will be taken to the 'themes gallery', just

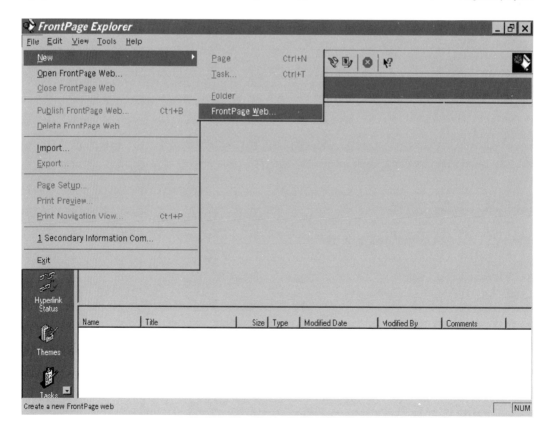

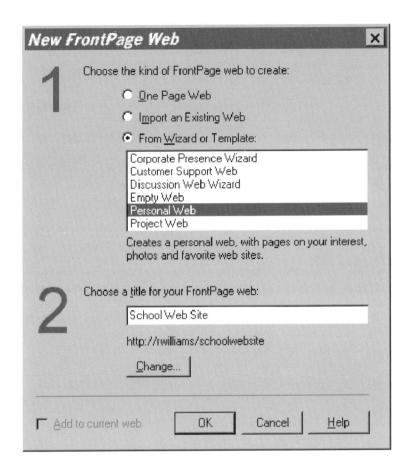

Fig. 71. Choosing a template which supports frames. There are lots of templates to choose from.

as in the last section where you created your own home page.

Choose the theme you want to go with and click 'Apply'. Then return to 'Navigation View' by hitting the appropriate button on the left.

What you have just done is apply a theme to the whole of your web site. When you add more pages to the site later on they too will have this theme. The great thing is that you can change the whole theme of your site at any time, just by running through that last procedure and choosing a different theme. Your whole site can be given a makeover in less than two minutes!

How do I remove pages and add banners?

Now it is time to get the rough architecture of your site in place so finding that piece of paper with the flow diagram would be a good idea.

The first difference Jim noticed is that his top page has only two links coming from it, whereas FrontPage has created a template that has three. One of those pages needs to go!

Let's get rid of the 'Favourites' page. Right-click over it to access the context-sensitive menu. As in Figure 72, select 'Delete'. You should then be presented with the 'Delete Page' dialogue box (Figure 73).

Adding pages to your site ....

Make sure that the radio button is checked so that you delete the actual files associated with that page from the site, and hit OK. You should then see that page disappear from the navigation view.

The next stage is to give these pages the correct names.

How do I give a page a name?

As mentioned earlier, FrontPage has built-in features to take advantage of frames. Wouldn't it be great if you could have a banner at the top of each page, telling you what the content was? No prizes for guessing that you can and it is really easy too.

Notice the titles of the three pages of your site; Home Page, Interests and Photo Album.

▷ Right-click over Home Page once and select 'Rename'.

▷ Then type in '[your school name] Web Site'.

▷ Carry out the same procedure for the other two, following the flow diagram that you sketched out earlier.

How do I add more pages to the site?

Fig. 72. Deleting existing web pages.

Look at the top-left of the screen. You should notice a button called 'New Page', just like the one in Figure 74. That is a really useful button and one you will be seeing a lot more of. Adding pages is easy.

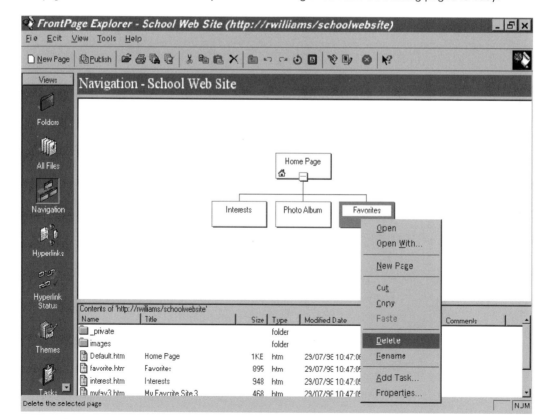

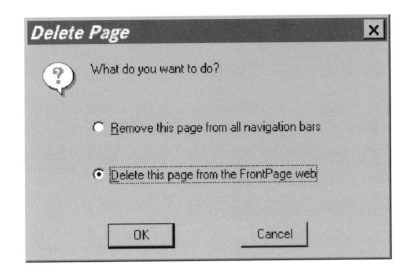

Fig. 73. Making sure the files are deleted too.

Simply select the page you want to link from with the left mouse button and then hit the 'New Page' button. In Figure 74 we have added two new pages from the 'Contact Information Page'. We have also renamed one of them 'Contact the Head Teacher' and the other 'Contact the Secretary'.

Do the same for the other pages in your site until it mirrors the structure of your flow diagram.

Fig. 74. The 'New Page' button.

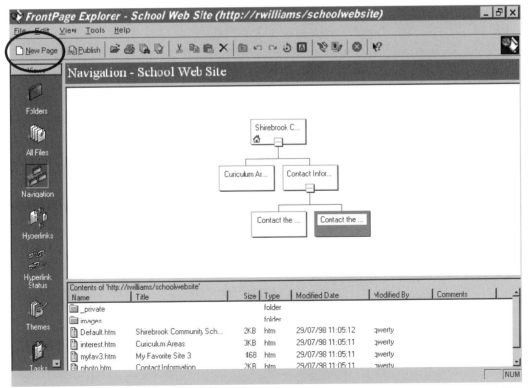

105

Making changes to the template ....

Finishing off the site

Now the large-scale structure of the site is done, all you need to do is add the content. As in the previous chapter, you now need to open up the FrontPage Editor. Add your text, pictures and links to make the site complete.

Remember, opening up the Editor is achieved by double-clicking the left mouse button on a page in Navigation view. When the Editor is opened you will see a page just like the one in Figure 75.

The text is there for guidance only, so start by getting rid of it.

In terms of layout, the page should reflect the three-frame concept explained earlier. Although it is now just a matter of adding content, there are one or two things you can do to make the site a little easier to use. Obviously it is up to you to decide whether you prefer these changes or not but we find them useful.

Making some slight changes to the template

The first thing to do is get rid of that navigation bar below the main banner.

Fig. 75. A web page opened up in FrontPage Editor.

▷ Right click on it and select 'cut'. Although it does go, you are left with a nasty gap in the page.

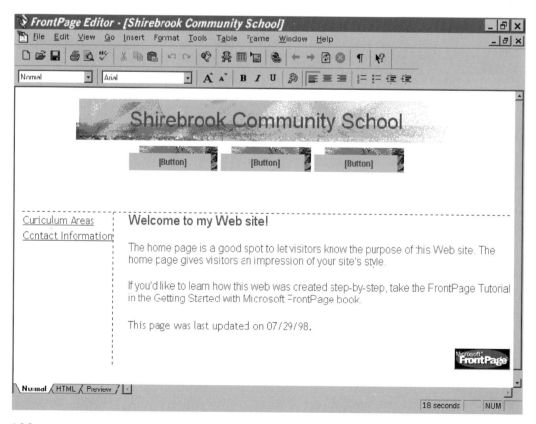

Use your cursor to close up this gap. You could even add a horizontal line in the space, by selecting Insert/Horizontal Line. This should make the page look more like the one in Figure 76. At the moment you will notice that the links on the left of the page are text-only (circled in Figure 76).

Now, wouldn't they look better as nice big buttons? That is easy to do, too.

▷ Right-click over the links and select FrontPage Component Properties. A dialogue box will appear, just like the one in Figure 77.

▷ Check the radio button that makes the links appear as buttons rather than text.

▷ Similarly, check the box that makes the buttons show the 'Parent page' too. This will make your site much easier to navigate.

Now that is done, switch between the Explorer and Editor views, adding the content to all your pages. Ensure that you periodically save the pages in the Editor view; just go to File/Save All.

Publishing your page on the web using Microsoft FrontPage can be done in just the same way as in Chapter 8, although it will take a bit longer!

Fig. 76. Finding the navigation bar.

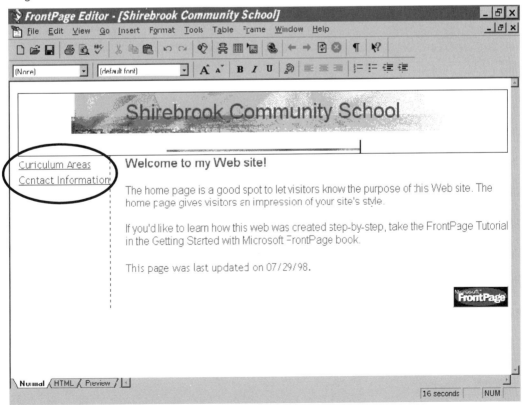

Fig. 77. Changing the navigation bar properties.

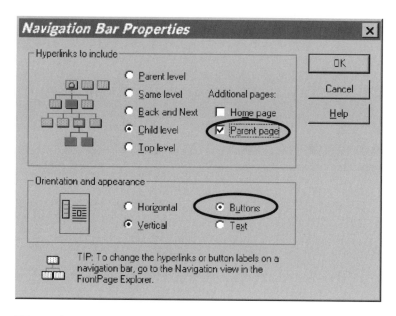

Managing the site

When the page is complete and online it is tempting to sit back and relax. However, just as with any other school publication, it is really important that you keep the site relevant and up-to-date so that it reflects the events and activities that are taking place in your school. A few simple changes in the content can make the site so much more useful not only to other users generally but also to parents in the catchment that you serve. What better way of promoting home–school links than via the school web site?

Similarly, when supported by regular feedback and material from other curriculum areas, the web site can become a really effective medium which parents, students and the public in general can access to find out just what positive things are taking place in your school.

Make sure you spend just a little time each term to ensure the page is accurate and contemporary.

Summary

In this chapter we have looked at how to design and build a web site with features and content that will add value to your school.

In the next chapter we will examine how to transfer data between computers using generic software and File Transfer Protocol.

10 Transferring files across the globe

In this chapter you will be introduced to the following topics:

▶ *what FTP is*
▶ *how to use FTP software*
▶ *some common problems encountered when FTP'ing web sites*
▶ *other uses of FTP.*

. . . .

What is FTP?

It is the ability to exchange information that makes the internet so powerful. File transfer protocol was briefly mentioned in Chapter 1 as one of the internet components that make this exchange possible. FTP was originally designed to meet the need to transfer large files from one point to another. It is one of the few early internet technologies that is still frequently used today.

How it works

In its simplest form FTP sends files between two computers. It can also remotely create, remove or rename directories and files.

First, we will examine how to use FTP software to send files from your computer to the computer of your internet provider. If you have used software such as Microsoft Publisher or Word97 to produce your home page, then you will need to 'ftp' your files in this way.

Remote and local

When talking of file transfer, you may hear the terms 'remote' and 'local' crop up quite often. They refer to the locations of the computers you are working with in relation to you. The computer that you use is local to you, whilst your internet provider's computer is remote.

Of course, this concept is reversed from their perspective!

What FTP software should we use?

The good news is that most FTP software is available either free (as freeware) or very cheaply (as shareware). Below are some examples of commonly used applications for carrying out FTP.

Most web browsers also let you download FTP programs from a remote computer, without having to use task-specific software. This is achieved through simply clicking on hyperlinks on web pages.

WS_FTP Explorer Pro
http://www.ipswitch.com/
This is a favourite of many users. It has a friendly graphical interface,

making transferring files much like copying using File Manager in Windows 3.11. Ipswitch Software allow you to download an evaluation version of WS_FTP from their web site.

CuteFTP
http://www.cuteftp.com/
This is another popular FTP program due to its Explorer-like interface. It uses simple drag-and-drop techniques to allow file transfer between sites. GlobalScape allow download of the software for evaluation from their site, too.

FTPVoyager
http://www.ftpvoyager.com/
This is a new FTP program which is gaining popularity very quickly, due to its truly Explorer-like interface. Again, drag-and-drop is used to transfer files easily. Deerfield.com allow a trial download of their shareware product from the URL shown above.

Using FTP

We will assume you are using WS_FTP, as it is fairly easy to use and will help you to learn some of the concepts involved.

Case study: Steve wants to upload his finished home page

Steve has just finished writing his home page using Microsoft Word 97. He now has a collection of files on his hard drive (**local**) that need transferring to his internet provider (**remote**). Since Word does not handle the FTP'ing, Steve will have to do it manually. He chooses WS_FTP Explorer Pro to do the job for him.

Setting up your FTP software step by step

Step 1

When you do this yourself, first of all note which directory (or 'folder') on your hard drive contains the files you want to upload. Write down the full path to this directory, which could look something like one of these:

C:\My Documents\My school website files

C:\FrontPage webs\Content.

Step 2

Connect to your internet service provider.

Step 3

Now run your WS_FTP software program. You should then see a dialogue box like the one in Figure 78.

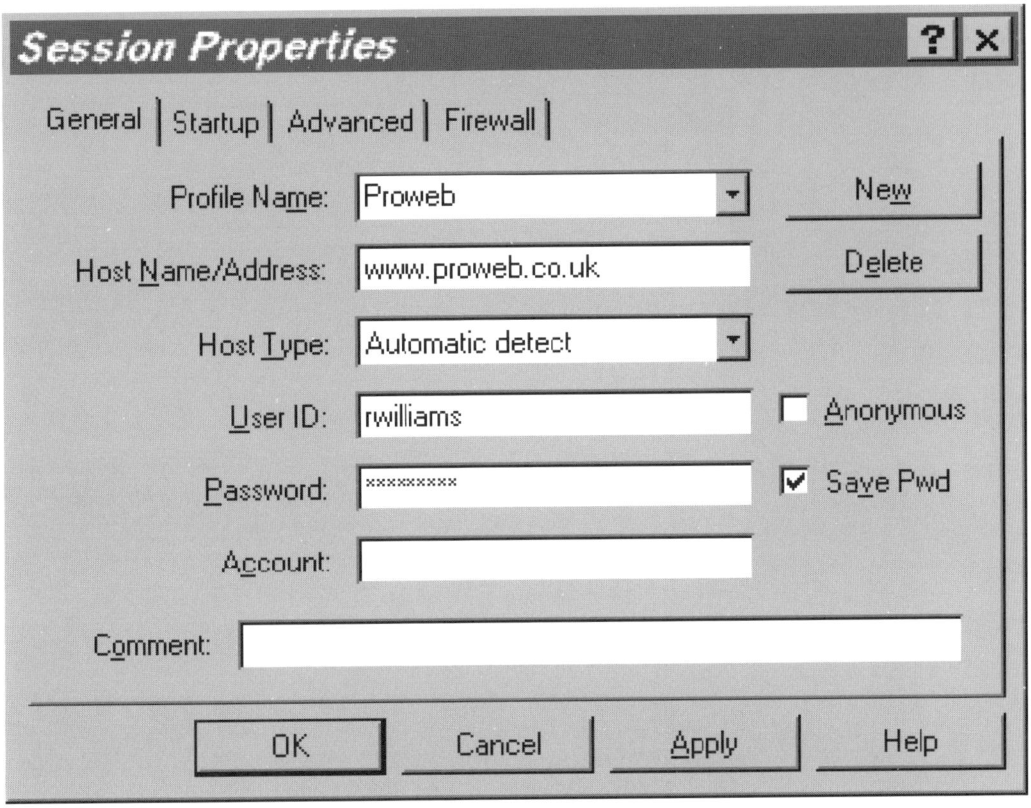

Session Properties

General | Startup | Advanced | Firewall

Profile Name: Proweb

Host Name/Address: www.proweb.co.uk

Host Type: Automatic detect

User ID: rwilliams ☐ Anonymous

Password: xxxxxxxxx ☑ Save Pwd

Account:

Comment:

New   Delete

OK   Cancel   Apply   Help

Do not be put off at this stage. It's quite easy to set up WS_FTP! You just have to fill in the text boxes with the correct information.

Fig. 78. Setting up the session properties in WS_FTP.

Here is what each piece of information means:

Profile name   The 'friendly' name for all this information,
                   which saves you typing it all in again later.

Host name/address The address of your internet provider's FTP
                   server. If you are unsure, do not worry.

Host type   Leave as it is – 'Autodetect'.

User ID   Your login name for your internet account.
                   Mine is 'rwilliams'.

Password   The password to give you access to your
                   internet account.

Account   Leave this blank.

An internet provider runs several servers, each involved with carrying out a different task. For example, one server deals with email (the mail server), another with web pages (the web server), and another with transferring files between computers using FTP (the FTP server).

What if I do not know any of the information needed?
More than likely you are unsure of the address of your internet provider's FTP server. However, guessing what to put should do. For a start it will begin with 'ftp'. What follows next is the domain name of

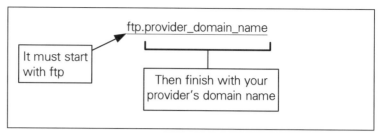

your internet provider, as in Figure 79. Take a look at the examples below and then take a guess.

Internet service provider	Hyperlink	FTP host name/address
Demon Internet	ftp://ftp.demon.co.uk	ftp.demon.co.uk
Easynet	ftp://ftp.easynet.co.uk	ftp.easynet.co.uk
Proweb	ftp://ftp.proweb.co.uk	ftp.proweb.co.uk

What if I don't know my User ID?
If you are unsure of what your 'User ID' is then it should be easy to find, too. From your Windows 95 or 98 desktop, hit:

Start button/ /Settings/Control Panel

Then from the list select 'Internet'. What should appear is a dialogue box like the one below.

Select the 'Connection' tab at the top, and then hit the 'Settings' button just below, circled on the diagram. What opens up is a dialogue box that contains your dial-up settings. The section labelled 'User' contains a

Fig. 80. The internet properties dialogue box.

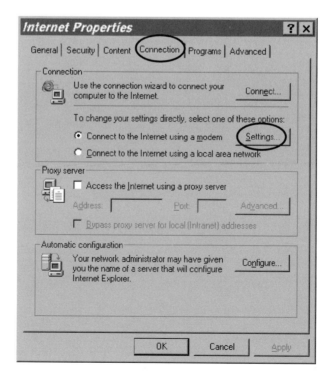

text box. This is your 'User ID' and needs to be entered into the WS_FTP dialogue box in the appropriate place.

What about my password?
You will notice that your password is starred out. Unfortunately if you do not know the password you are not going to be able to FTP up to your disk space. Contact your internet provider directly if you are unsure.

Step 4

Once you have hit the 'OK' button, the software will establish a connection with the FTP server owned by your internet provider. It will then open up the main window in which you will be working (see Figure 81).

Transferring your files

Let us take some time to get more familiar with that important window

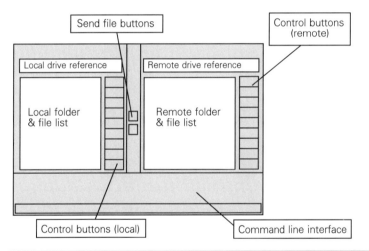

Fig. 81. The main WS_FTP window.

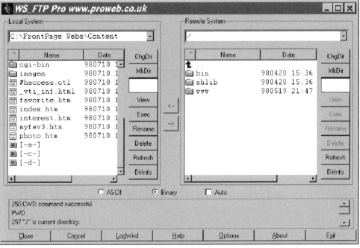

Uploading to a remote computer.................................

in Figure 81. It is from here that most of the file transfers will be managed.

The window can be split into two, with details of the local machine (yours) on the left and the remote machine (your internet provider's) on the right.

▷ With reference to Figure 81, the **local** machine shows folders and files that are in c:\FrontPage webs\Content.

▷ The **remote** machine on the right shows just three folders in the root directory – bin, shlib and www.

In a moment we will transfer (send copies of) the two folders and seven files from the local computer into the 'www' folder on the host. The first step is opening up the 'www' folder at the host, ready to drop those folders and files into. To do this requires navigating through the directory structure of the remote computer's hard drive.

Navigating around the remote computer

Just like navigating around your own computer, use the mouse pointer to double-click on the folder you want to open – 'www' in this case on the remote machine. That will open up that folder and display its contents in the right-hand frame, as in Figure 82.

As you can see, it is empty, containing no files or folders. Incidentally, to move back up the directory structure, double-click on the green arrow (circled below).

Fig. 82. Navigating around a remote machine.

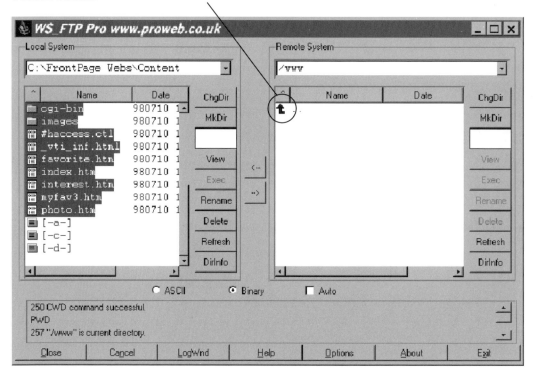

Selecting and uploading your files

The next stage is to select all the files on your local system that you want to transfer to the remote host (**upload**).

1. Browse your hard drive using the mouse pointer in the left-hand section of the WS_FTP window. Locate the files and folders you want to transfer.

2. Click on the first filename in the list. Then press the 'Shift' key on your keyboard and select the last in the list. This will highlight a whole column of folders and files, saving you from having to highlight them individually.

3. Finally, using the two 'Send file' buttons located in the centre of the window, send the files to the remote computer (the > arrow). When confirmed, WS_FTP will kick into action and transfer all of the files. Be patient though, as it could take a few minutes, depending on how many files you are sending, and how big they are.

Downloading files from the remote computer

Transferring files in the other direction uses the reverse procedure:

1. Open up the directory on the local computer that you want the files to download into.

2. Then select the files on the remote computer that you want to copy.

3. Finally hit the 'Send file' button (this time the < arrow).

What if I send the wrong files?
Deleting files on the host is no problem. Just highlight the file to delete and hit the appropriate control button on the right-hand side (delete). The host will instantly delete the file automatically.

Checking that your files are now on the web

Once all your files have been transferred to the remote host computer, they should be viewable by anyone on the world wide web. How to check:

▷ Open up your web browser.

▷ Type in the URL of your site.

Your home page should now appear – congratulations!

If you cannot seem to access your site, look at the list of most common causes of problems below, and try the solution suggested.

Possible problems . . . .

Common problems when FTP'ing web pages

Do not panic just because you cannot seem to access your site! Computers are prone to not doing what you want them to, even if you have only made one tiny mistake. It is more than likely that by remedying that mistake you will solve the problem quickly.

▶ *Problem 1 – You have typed in the wrong URL for your site*

Check that the address that you keyed into your browser is the correct one for your site and in lower case. If you are unsure of what the URL is, look at the information your internet provider posted to you when you opened the account. Alternatively visit their web site and ask.

▶ *Problem 2 – You have not given your 'index' page the right filename*

When someone visits your site the first page your browser tries to open has the filename 'index.htm'. If you have not given your top or welcome page that filename, your browser will not be happy and will return an error. Use WS_FTP to rename the file if necessary.

▶ *Problem 3 – You have FTP'd into the wrong directory on the remote computer*

In the FTP example above, the files were transferred into the folder called 'www' on the host computer. This is because it is in this folder that a user's web pages are kept and accessed. If they had been put into any of the other folders, then the host's web server would not be able to find them, and the user would receive an error. Make sure you put the files into the correct place. If unsure ask your internet provider.

Other uses of FTP

It is not just the files that go to make up a web site that can be FTP'd, but files of any type, including documents, applications, images, sound files and so on. Obviously the bigger the file is, the longer it takes to transfer from one computer to another. It follows therefore that the more expensive it is to upload or download.

Zipping and unzipping files

Quite often to minimise the size of files they are 'zipped up' or compressed before transfer, and then 'unzipped' or decompressed afterwards. Special compression software is used to perform these tasks. The most common one is **WinZip**.

A shareware utility, WinZip is fairly easy to use. It contains a great tutorial which leads you through the process of zipping and unzipping files step by step.

> **Tip**
>
> Remember that if you put large files onto your web site for others to download, it is standard procedure to zip them up beforehand!

116

Summary

In this chapter we have looked at how to transfer files from a remote computer to a host computer using specialised software. We have also looked at some commonly experienced problems which can prevent a web page being accessed, and identified solutions to them. In the next chapter we will look at the advantages of setting up an **intranet** within a school environment.

Fig. 83. You can download a copy of WS_FTP from Ipswitch.com.

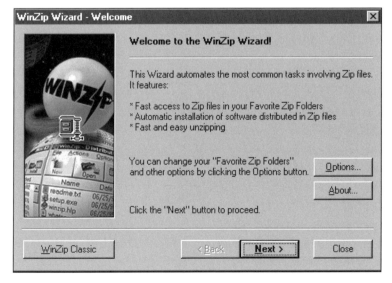

Fig. 84. What WinZip looks like on your computer screen when you are ready to zip or unzip files.

11 Launching your school intranet

In this chapter you will be introduced to the following topics:

▶ *what an 'intranet' is*
▶ *the potential of intranets in the school environment*
▶ *how to design and build an effective intranet*
▶ *how to manage an intranet.*

· ·

So, what is an intranet?

Not more terminology! It is always the same with computers – you learn all about a new feature or concept and then just around the corner there seems to be yet another mountain to climb.

But try not to worry because you are already half way there with this one. Much of what you have learned in the rest of the book about the internet applies to intranets too, so persevere because it will be worth it.

Intranet defined

An intranet is a private computer network that uses internet standards and protocols to enable members of an organisation to communicate with each other much more efficiently.

Basically it is like having your very own mini version of the internet within the school. Only you can access it, and it only contains content that you approve of. The benefits sound great already, but before moving on, let us compare the internet and intranets in more detail.

Question and answer

What are the differences between the internet and an intranet?
Look at the table below.

Internet	Intranet
Not owned by any individual	Owned by the organisation which hosts it
Anyone can access it	Only those given access rights can browse
Can be accessed from anywhere	Runs on a single site
Contains much unsuitable content	Contains only specified content

There are, however, many more similarities than differences:

▷ both use pages written in HTML

▷ both use web browsers to view these pages

▷ both use the same standards and protocols to distribute the data over a network.

This brings some great benefits that we can explore in more detail later. Now that you are a little more aware of what an intranet is, let us look at how schools can benefit.

What is the potential of a school intranet?

Like any organisation, a school relies strongly on effective communication between individuals. As every teacher knows, it is this sharing of information that facilitates learning amongst the student body.

An intranet can enhance this sharing of information. This is because you decide what the content is. As we will see later, an intranet can also be used to collect useful information from the students. With intranets the movement of information is a two-way street.

Some basic intranet ideas

Clearly an intranet can contain information on a diverse range of topics and below are some specific ideas that apply particularly to schools.

Curriculum content guides

Imagine having pages that tell the students exactly what they will be studying next week, next term or even next year. Putting your Programmes of Study on an intranet empowers the students by giving them the opportunity to read ahead for upcoming lessons, improving their time management.

Extension materials and activities

As mentioned earlier, intranet pages are written in HTML, just like web pages, so you can easily transfer pages from the world wide web to your intranet site!

▷ *Example* – Imagine a school intranet site that contains a Geography section. This term the Year 9s are studying Natural Hazards and specifically Earthquakes. You could find an internet page about the Kobe earthquake and put it onto the Year 9 Geography section of your intranet.

News and events

An intranet is a really effective way of keeping both staff and students informed of what is going on within the school. This can be achieved by incorporating your school calendar into the site, along with a brief news section.

Setting up an intranet..

Data collection

The technology behind intranets makes data collection really easy to build into your school site. The only limit is your imagination. Such interactivity allows many topics to be covered.

▷ *Example* – a competition could be run requiring the students to submit their answers via a form on the intranet. Or how about a page dedicated to collecting confidential information from students about bullying incidents?

Obviously the list could go on and on. The key point is that an intranet has all the benefits of the internet but can be tailored to suit your particular school's needs.

Do not worry too much about the logistics of setting up an intranet. Although it seems like a daunting task it is really as easy as writing pages for the world wide web.

How do I set up an intranet?

You are probably setting up this project from scratch, so really ensure that what you do will add value to your school. This will be more likely if you take some time in the design stages to identify exactly what you want your intranet to achieve.

Case studies

▷ *The curricular route* – Quite a few students in Chris's school regularly ask for extension work. This tends to be problematic in terms of teacher time. Chris therefore decides that these students would benefit if they were given easy access to the Programmes of Study in an attractive environment. Associated with each term's work are extension activities that the students can access at any time, therefore ensuring the students are stretched to their full potential.

▷ *The communication route* – In contrast Harry feels that communication between the staff and students could improve, because students often do not know what events are taking place. His intranet solution is to design a site that has a calendar of events for the year, including extra-curricular activities taking place each week. He also believes that giving the students their own section on the intranet will give the staff some insight into the goings on within the student body.

These two intranet sites have very different content, suited to the individual schools. Chris's intranet would not necessarily work in Harry's school, and vice versa.

Make sure that your site is designed to hold useful content that will add value to your institution.

.... Incorporating pages from the world wide web

Putting pen to paper

Designing the layout of an intranet is almost identical to designing your school web site, which we explored in the previous chapter.

▷ Starting with an index or 'Welcome' page at the top, design all of the sub-pages that your intranet site will contain.

▷ Again, it is really important to be realistic and not over-ambitious at first. Remember that you can always add more later. Producing a large site too soon will really eat away at your valuable time!

Once the site has been designed, follow the same procedures as in Chapters 8 and 9. Producing an attractive intranet site using software such as Microsoft FrontPage is relatively simple. Do make sure you remember exactly where it is on your hard-drive, as you will need to transfer it across to the server at some point.

Before that though, what would you do to incorporate web pages into your intranet site?

Incorporating pages from the world wide web

To get pages from the web to your intranet you need to physically grab them and put them onto the hard drive of your computer. This process is known as **web-whacking**. It can be done really easily using FrontPage.

1. Load the FrontPage Explorer. If the 'Getting Started' dialogue box appears hit the 'Cancel' button, as in Figure 85 below.

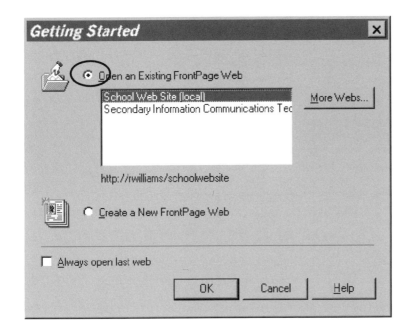

Fig. 85. Opening an existing web page.

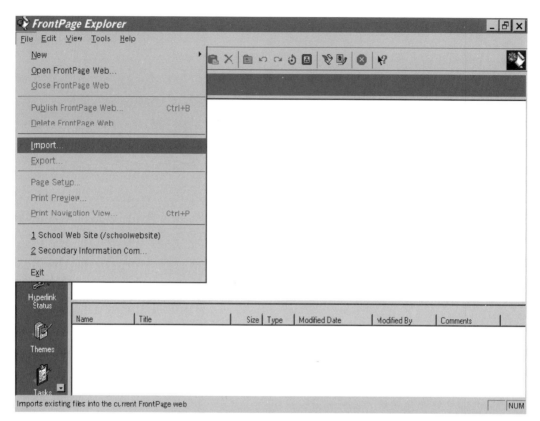

Fig. 86. Importing a web page . . .

Fig. 87. . . . that already exists.

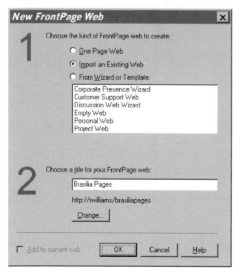

2. Next, minimise FrontPage and access your dial-up account with your internet provider. Once you are online, use Internet Explorer to find the URL of the site that you want to grab.

3. Returning to the FrontPage Explorer, select File/Import, as in Figure 86. You will see the dialogue box captured in Figure 87. Make sure the radio button is selected to 'import an existing web'. Then give the page a name, which it will appear as on your hard drive. In this example it is 'Brasilia Pages'.

4. After hitting 'OK', another dialogue box will pop up, asking you where to get the page from (Figure 88). Choose 'From a World Wide Web site'. In the text box type in the exact URL of the site. Then hit 'Next'.

5. Yet another box appears, as in Figure 89. This time it is asking how many levels below your title page you want to go. We would recommend about 3 or 4, so key in this information and click 'Next' and then 'Finish'. FrontPage will then set to work whacking your page onto your hard drive.

5. Finally it is simply a matter of copying the file into the same area as your intranet and adding the pages to your existing structure. Whilst the web-whacked page is in the FrontPage Editor, take the

122

time to delete any links to pages that will not be on your intranet site.

How do I make my site available to the students?
With a web page you simply upload your site to your internet provider and let them worry about the rest. It may be worth knowing that the opposite of downloading – uploading – is transferring data from your computer to a host, usually your internet provider. With an intranet you have to set up your own computer to distribute the files requested by the students. This computer is known as a **web server**.

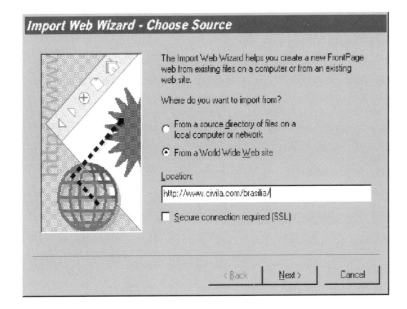

Fig. 88. Locating the site to import.

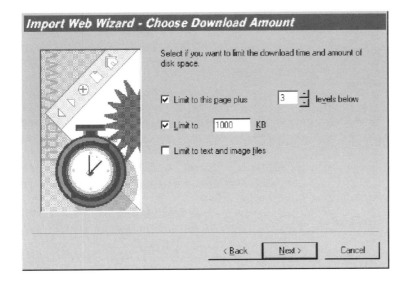

Fig. 89. Selecting how many levels of a site to import.

After the site has gone online......................................

Server application programs reside on this server, managing the various jobs that servers generally do. These include:

▷ processing mail

▷ storing data files

▷ sending appropriate data to users who request it from client terminals.

The server software is platform-specific. Windows NT, for example, uses different server software from a UNIX server. Fortunately most servers run TCP/IP. This effectively means it can distribute and gather information over your intranet.

Web server programs

You will need to get hold of a piece of software called a **web server program**, which must suit the type of server that you have. Many are available at no cost (as freeware) for many platforms. An example is **FastTrack** from the Netscape educational web page. The associated documentation explains the procedure you follow to get your project out to the users. It really is a lot simpler than you might think.

Help is at hand

If you feel that you do not have the confidence or time to write an entire intranet site from scratch, it may be worth knowing that Research Machines provide templates to schools who subscribe to their educational support services. Similar in concept to their school web site templates, the intranet templates have been carefully designed to meet the specific needs and opportunities opened up by a school intranet. Visit the **RM Eduweb** pages to find out more.

Managing an intranet

So the site is online, being used by lots of students and everyone is really impressed by your superhuman efforts. Like any major project this will require regular evaluation and update. Intranets need looking after very carefully.

We looked at how a web site needs regular reviews. That applies even more so to an intranet. Your audience has grown up in a sophisticated multimedia era of sound bites and information overload; they will expect regular updates to the content of the intranet.

Including information from the students is another good method of sustaining their continuing interest. It is also a fantastic way of getting the students working collaboratively.

For such a project to work you will need the students to be:

▷ journalists

▷ reporters

▷ page-designers

▷ writers

– a diverse range of skills. The key point is that the intranet is only a useful tool if it enhances the exchange of knowledge and information within the school. Your web server should enable you to see the statistics of how often the intranet is accessed during a day, week or term. If it does not seem to be working, try another approach!

Summary

In this chapter we have looked at the benefits a carefully designed intranet site can bring to a school, along with some ideas to include within such a site. We then examined how to design and build such a site, incorporating pages from the world wide web. We finished by thinking about the importance of keeping the site relevant and up to date.

In the next chapter we will look to the future, trying to identify ways in which the internet will influence education, along with ways in which you as a teacher can get involved.

12 A glimpse of the future

In this chapter you will be introduced to the following topics:

▶ *the National Grid for Learning*
▶ *accessing the school intranet from home*
▶ *distance learning*
▶ *teaching and learning resources on the internet.*

The National Grid for Learning (NGfL)

So what is the NGfL that I keep reading about?

No doubt you have read or heard about the NGfL in one form or another (Figure 90). Despite that, in many teachers' minds it remains a mystical beast! Basically the NGfL was born as a result of the government's commitment to modernising the education system in Britain. They say that to achieve this would mean 'making the most of technological change'.

Fig. 90. The National Grid for Learning.

Essentially there are three main elements to the NGfL:

▷ 'The Grid' is a collection of web pages which constitute resources and advice for use in education. These resources are accessible via the internet and, at the time of writing, the site consists of more than 60 000 pages of information and is growing rapidly.

▷ The government is equipping schools with the hardware necessary to access the Grid, via funding from the DfEE.

▷ Finally, the NGfL is to include an extensive training programme to help teachers and librarians with using IT in an educational context. This aspect of the NGfL is administered by the Teacher Training Agency (TTA), along with the Library and Information Commission (LIC).

Let's take a look at the Grid, the NGfL web site, and see what information is currently available online. At present there are four components or 'areas' to the site, each with a separate function:

▷ The Virtual Teacher Centre (VTC)

▷ The Standards and Effectiveness Database

▷ The Governors Centre

▷ The FE Hub.

Let's look at the function of each aspect of the NGfL web site.

The Virtual Teacher Centre (VTC)

The Virtual Teacher Centre (Figure 91) is based on five 'rooms':

▷ reception

▷ library

▷ meeting room

▷ classroom resources

▷ professional development.

The individual rooms are reached by clicking on the appropriate link. Although still in the prototype stages, the VTC is maintained by British Educational Communications and Technology Agency (BECTA).

The current content of the VTC is made up of web-based resource materials developed with public funds. This includes the:

(a) Curriculum IT Support (CITS) initiative

(b) Education Department's Superhighways Initiative (EDSI)

(c) Literacy Time

(d) Information for Senior Managers

(e) Lingu@NET – a virtual language centre.

The VTC also contains links to government and government-funded resources throughout the UK. Future targets of the NGfL will be explained in more detail later.

Fig. 91. The Virtual Teacher Centre.

NGfL in the future

The Standards and Effectiveness Database

This database aims to help schools to improve effectiveness and raise their standards, by providing 'succinct guidance, good illustrations of development in schools and research and inspection evidence' (Figure 92).

Fig. 92. The Standards and Effectiveness Database.

The site is rapidly becoming much more extensive, with both the range of topics covered and the functions available expanding as the site develops. The database currently has links to a great deal of material produced by the DfEE, such as guidance on summer schools, literacy, teacher appraisal, advice on the National Literacy Strategy and so on.

Fig. 93. The Governors Centre.

The Governors Centre

This section of the VTC acts as a resource for school governors. It contains information on topics such as responsibilities, good practice and how to become a school governor. This too is intended to be developed in the future once the NGfL moves beyond the prototype stages (Figure 93).

Fig. 94. The FE Hub.

The FE Hub

Finally, the FE Hub offers course leaders and tutors access to a range of curriculum and technical information regarding further education courses. There is also a links section to the latest news and press releases pertinent to this phase (Figure 94).

How will the NGfL web site develop in the future?

The NGfL web site is rapidly evolving into a powerful information hub giving access to a diverse range of useful information, all aimed at raising educational standards. However, it also encourages communication between all those involved in education, using the internet to its full potential towards this goal. In general, the web site will evolve to include the following:

(a) schemes of work for curriculum subjects

(b) examples of high quality material used by practising teachers, such as school behaviour plans and individual education plans.

In addition, there is information and guidance on government policy on a variety of subjects including:

▷ the national literacy and numeracy strategies
▷ raising standards and effectiveness
▷ school management
▷ school finance
▷ teacher supply, training and qualifications
▷ discipline and attendance
▷ special educational needs
▷ equal opportunities
▷ under-five provision
▷ out-of-school activities.

So the NGfL web site will be the resource and advice centre which should help schools make the most of the internet connections provided by the government. Make sure you spend some time visiting the pages, familiarising yourself with what each section has to offer.

Accessing the school intranet from home

In the last chapter we introduced the idea of intranets. We explained that they could be accessed by privileged users upon a local area network.

Although that is true, an intranet can *also* be accessed via a dial-up connection from home. When this occurs, the intranet becomes an **extranet**. Think of it as an extension to the existing intranet, to which only certain people (such as parents) can gain access.

How does the extranet work?

It is possible to have your extranet data on your internet provider's hard-drive. However, this can create problems with security and keeping your intranet and extranet the same. A simpler approach is to allow users to access the intranet data on the school web server via a dial-up connection. This has the advantages of:

▷ reducing security problems

▷ eliminating the headache of having two sets of the same data to manage.

Extranet advantages

Extranets open up many new exciting opportunities for schools. Their strength lies in the fact that they are only accessible to individuals who are given access. Clearly this is an advantage where schools are concerned. It is widely accepted, and obviously good practice, not to include sensitive information upon a school web site, since this information could potentially endanger individual students.

However, because an extranet is not a publicly accessible resource it is entirely feasible to include such information as content upon the pages. The examples below suggest some information that would be useful to include upon an intranet, but not suitable to include on a web site:

▷ details of a trip that is taking place, including times and equipment needed

▷ a 'well-done' section detailing individual students' achievements

▷ information about a parents' evening, with the facility to make bookings.

Most computers are now being marketed and sold as 'internet ready'. This basically means they arrive with a modem installed, and the relevant browser software on CD-ROM. With more and more families now owning such a PC, it is important for schools to understand the potential that a well written and relevant extranet could have in encouraging home–school links.

Distance learning

'Distance learning' is a general term used to cover the broad range of teaching and learning events in which the student is separated (at a distance) from the teacher, or other fellow learners.

▷ It is highly likely that within five years your school will be offering at least A-level and GNVQ courses via the internet.

In order to undertake a distance learning programme, the following facilities will be required by both the students and teachers:

(a) a dial-up connection to an internet provider (ISDN if possible)

(b) a web browser

(c) a mail and news reader

(d) video-conferencing hardware and software

What is video-conferencing?

The term video-conferencing is used to describe *live* audio and video communication between at least two individuals using the internet. This usually takes place with each participant using a microphone and small camera to exchange audio and video data, which allows real-time communication via the internet.

Video-conferencing allows communication not only between two individuals but also between larger groups of people. This opens up many communication possibilities within the context of an online course. For example, a teacher could deliver a lecture to a small group of students or debrief an individual student on a piece of coursework at a distance.

Case study
Miss Smith is giving an A-level physics lesson using video-conferencing technology to a small group of six students *each in their own homes.* Not only can the students see and hear her, they can also see diagrams she is using in Microsoft PowerPoint to illustrate a difficult concept. Because they are 'sharing' the PowerPoint program, they can ask her questions in real-time and point to various features on the slide using their mouse. The good thing is that they all see and hear what is going on, just like a real lesson.

Think of the benefits of offering such a course in catchments that currently do not contain sufficient numbers to make post-16 education financially feasible.

Video-conferencing used to support students

In the future it is envisaged that video-conferencing will be a much more widely available feature of schools and homes than it is at present. The technology will be a key area in which students can gain educational support.

Schools will be able to pay a subscription to an independent company offering online educational support 24 hours a day, and the students within the school will be given access to a range of 'experts' online.

Using video-conferencing technology the student will contact the organisation's server via a dial-up connection and from there contact one of the subject specialists currently online.

Video-conferencing and whiteboard technology

Many of us teach using whiteboards within the classroom. In IT, however, a **whiteboard** means a piece of hardware that combines all the features of a conventional whiteboard with the multimedia advantages of a computer. This allows diagrams, graphs, text and animations to be displayed to a class (Figure 95).

Using a fast internet connection it is already possible for two institutions to share a whiteboard presentation. It is hoped that the future will see much more of this technology within educational institutions. The scenario would involve a guest lecturer giving a talk, with classes around the world hearing the audio on speakers, whilst seeing the diagrams or animations on a whiteboard at the front of the class.

How will distance learning affect schools?
Offering students courses via the internet could have a huge impact on schools and colleges within the UK – and every other country in the

Fig. 95. Whiteboard technology.

world. One particular problem facing many schools today is that there are insufficient numbers within travelling distance of the school to make setting up post-16 education feasible.

Distance learning removes the spatial factor from this equation, opening up the institution to a potentially global body of students.

It is very likely that in the near future many schools will be offering courses not just to attending students, but to 'virtual' students too. These virtual students will be from other parts of the UK – even from other countries. They will submit work via email attachments, keep up to date via newsgroups, and attend lessons via video-conferencing. Likewise, the course teacher will use the internet to disseminate information, collect coursework, provide feedback and deliver material.

Teaching and learning resources on the internet

The internet gives access to a massive amount of knowledge and information on a huge range of topics. Consequently it has great potential as a resource for teachers and students. At present the quality of that information is very good. In the future it will be excellent.

Already teachers have access to a diverse range of material for use in the classroom, such as that from the Pearson Publishing site (see Appendix). The internet will reduce the need to order inspection or preview copies of resources. For example, at the Pearson site teachers can download example worksheets and classroom activities.

An increase in the range of material available online should drive up the standards of the classroom resources we use. Clearly the internet can only offer us far more choice in the resources we use.

Mailing lists and newsgroups will also develop towards meeting educational needs in the future. It is envisaged that specific lists and groups will arise to meet the needs of the new Advanced Skills Teachers over the next year or so, to provide a forum where collaboration and the sharing of ideas can take place.

Keeping in touch via the internet is a tremendously efficient and effective way of ensuring that good practice is shared amongst such professionals.

What it means for teachers

For you this will mean that the internet, or more specifically, the world wide web, will be a fantastic source of information for use within your lessons. You will be able to download worksheets directly or construct them yourself using snippets of text and diagrams from the web. Similarly you could give the students within your class access to the web directly, using the online material as a learning aid. It also means that you will be able to share ideas using increasingly focused newsgroups and mailing lists.

What it means for students

For the student, access to such a wealth of information can only be a good thing. High level research and information-processing skills will be vital for students of the future, as they trawl through the available content looking for the right pieces of information. Not only that, but actively seeking out information from the pertinent organisations or individual makes learning exciting and contemporary for the student. It is also expected that secure newsgroups and mailing lists will emerge for students too. In fact, as the subject develops, the teaching of information-handling skills within IT will become increasingly significant or perhaps even dominant over the development of IT software-handling skills.

Also in the future, we can expect to see much more sharing of information between schools. With each school owning its own web space and with staff having access to an internet connection, communication between schools will be much easier.

Similarly the transfer of curriculum resources in electronic form will revolutionise cross-educational links and consortia.

Summary

In this chapter we have looked at the development of the National Grid for Learning in the UK, along with how it is hoped it will evolve in the future. We have also considered some of the ways in which the internet will enhance education by making information-sharing easier to carry out.

Recommended reading and resources

. . . .

Books

It is difficult to recommend books in general since they apt to go out of date. Moreover, many books on the internet have a US bias and the US price translated into pounds means that these books are often very expensive. Other titles in the Internet Handbook series will be worth perusing, as the aim is to keep them up to date and reasonably priced. The series also has its own web site at:

http://www.internet-handbooks.co.uk

Magazines

Computer magazines are burgeoning on the shelves of many newsagents. Most have more advertising than content, and much of the content is mainly of consumer interest or targeted to the popular entertainment interests of the 'youth market'.

However, there are some magazines worth trying. The following have been found quite useful. Most are published monthly and cost around £3 or so.

Title	Publisher
.Net	Future
Internet@ccess made easy	Paragon
PC Pro	Dennis
Personal Computer World	VNU

Web sites

There are so many web sites with their own internet guides of one kind or another that it would be hard to review them all. As well as the sites mentioned in this book try these:

http://www.learnthenet.com
Definitely one of the best tutorials.

http://www.bbc.co.uk/
Computers Don't Bite site: teachers pages.

http://easyweb.easynet.co.uk/~etfreedman
Lots of links to IT materials: a great site.

http://rs.internic.net/nic-support/15min
Brilliant '15 minute' PowerPoint presentations.

Newspapers

The following quality newspapers all have useful supplements published each week:

Title	Website	Published
Guardian	www.guardiangp.co.uk	Thursday
Times	www.the-times.co.uk	Wednesday
Independent	www.independent.co.uk	Tuesday
Sunday Times	www.sunday-times.co.uk	Sunday *Innovation* section
Observer	www.guardian.co.uk	Sunday
Telegraph	www.telegraph.co.uk	Thursday

Appendix: Web sites for schools

. . . .

CHAPTER 1

What is the internet and why use it?

BBC Education Page

http://www.bbc.co.uk/education
This page has links to the BBC's main education pages as well as up-to-date information on the latest educational programmes on the BBC channels. Links take you to the BBC Learning Station, a service for primary and secondary teachers, the BBC Learning Zone and FE pages and the *Computers Don't Bite* site which contains pages directly aimed at teachers. You can also receive a weekly email from BBC Education with latest news of this site and BBC educational programmes.

BBC Education Web Guide

http://www.bbc.co.uk/
The Web Guide contains a selection of educational web sites reviewed by a team of educationalists. Sites for primary and secondary schools must fulfil the needs of the National Curriculum. Teachers can recommend sites that can join the database. Searches can be by key words and also allow Boolean operators – AND, OR and NOT. The site is catalogued in a simple directory format.

BECTA

http://www.becta.org.uk
The British Educational Communications and Technology Agency (BECTA) is the new name for the National Council for Educational Technology. Content is divided into several major categories:

Information
Education news.
Information sheets.
Summaries of OFSTED documents on IT.
Press releases and information on censorship issues, filtering and modems.

Internet projects
European initiatives.
Ling@NET – excellent resource for language teachers.
Multimedia projects, awards, SENCO support and Teacher Training.

Resources
Full text of publications.
CD-ROM reviews.
Advice on video-conferencing, ESL and SEN, the millennium bug and support providers.

CampusWorld

http://www.campus.bt.com/CampusWorld/

BT's educational internet service. Most of it is a *walled garden* that can only be accessed by subscribers. Contains training materials, web directories and a mass of projects for schools to get involved in along with some curriculum and materials and links, which are unique to the site. Customers are offered various levels of connection including HomeCampus for the domestic user.

Channel4

http://www.schools.channel4.com

Mostly supports the network's educational programmes. The teachers' forum is very quiet! Science materials and online experiments are noteworthy.

Department for Education and Employment

http://www.dfee.gov.uk

The government's Education and Employment ministry site. Contains a mass of information:

   for parents
   on education and training
   equal opportunities
   for schools and governors
   for job seekers
   for employers
   recent press releases.

A good place to find the latest pronouncements on education including White Papers such as *Excellence in Schools*. Also the place the find out the current thinking on the *Information Superhighway*! Performance tables can be accessed here as well.

Educate Online

http://www.educate.co.uk

A good collection of resources for teachers and a market for some leading educational publishers and suppliers.

The European Schoolnet

http://www.eun.org

Good place to find out what's happening in the European Union. Sponsored by the EU, the site contains a virtual teacher college with materials that aid teachers' professional development. *See* **Web for Schools Project** site below.

The Global Schoolhouse

http://www.gsn.org

This site is sponsored by Microsoft and contains some materials difficult to find elsewhere. It has three main areas:

Web sites for schools ....

The Connected Educator
This contains:
Teacher activity guides
Encarta Schoolhouse
Online software guides
Global Schoolnet projects, listservs and training solutions.

The Connected Classroom
Here you can:
Register for class projects and see what projects have been taking place throughout the world.
Create and publish web pages.

The Connected Learning Community
Make contact with other schools and institutions that are using new technologies to the full.

Kathy Schrock's Guide for Educators
http://www.capecod.net/schrockguide/
This site describes itself as a categorised list of sites on the internet found to be useful for enhancing curriculum and teachers' professional growth. It is updated daily. It contains:

A subject directory with links to web sites.
Links to major search engines and online guides.
Additional information referring to:

Training slide shows
Recommended books and software and
Information on workshops.

Northern Ireland Network for Education
http://www.nine.org.uk
Easy to use and not just for teachers in Northern Ireland. Structured through subjects and key stages.

Putnam Valley – Developing Educational Standards
http://199.224.4.2/Standards.html
Inspired by *Goals2000: Educate America Act*.
This URL contains annotated links to sites, which contain materials that focus on educational standards and curriculum frameworks. The site is classified by US state, subject area, country and organisation. The aim is to use the internet to make this information easily available to teachers in an indexed form.

SCET
http://www.scet.com
Scottish schools IT advice centre. The site hosts details of the courses it runs, its annual conference, software it produces or recommends and a list of Scottish schools online. The Technology Centre contains information on the teaching of IT. The *Latest Educational News* section

contains just that, plus SCET's responses to government papers such as the *Public Libraries IT Network*.

The School Page UK

http://www.eyesoftime.com/teacher/ukpage.htm
The site contains links to web sites and help from resident experts – mostly practising teachers who respond to queries via email. There is also an email-based newsletter that allows teachers to receive the latest updates of the site.

TeacherGridUK

http://www.teachergrid.com/index.html
This site is sponsored by BT, Microsoft and Research Machines. At present it has five main sections:

Curriculum Resources
Some resources culled here from CampusWorld.

Teacher Training
Not much here yet but this could become more interesting with the start of the teacher training program for 2002. Links to Microsoft's educational pages for school managers and BT's book on the internet are included.

Live Events
These take place monthly and include interviews with key personalities on current items of interest.

Discussion Groups
These are mainly from the RM site and not very active compared with Usenet.

Education News
Regular news from the three main sponsors.

Fig. 96. Teacher Grid.

Web sites for schools ....

TeachNet.com
http://www.teachnet.com
US site that provides a large number of lesson plans catalogued in directory format, plus tips for the day – some of which are very good! The site also hosts Teacher2Teacher links and provides free computer manuals for schools. There is also a KeyPals project here.

Uksforum
http://members.aol.com/uksforum/webguide
There are links here to a host of educational sites. Some of these are difficult to find elsewhere. An introduction to the site is found in a *Quick Trip for Teachers*.

UltraLab
http://www.ultralab.anglia.ac.uk/
This site is an educational technology learning research centre at Anglia Polytechnic University, Chelmsford. Its splendid aim is to: 'research, apply and disseminate the benefits of new technologies, seeking to develop and empowering a creative and delightful learning environment that knows no boundaries'. The site contains an up-to-date news section and links to major educational sites including the host of a full copy of the Stevenson Report on ICT in UK schools. There are papers related to UltraLab itself and links to sites and projects it supports. UltraLab supports the following projects (amongst others): TeacherNet (q.v.), the New Millennium Experience Company and Learning Zone (part of the Millennium Dome), One eMail per pupil, and notschool.net (a virtual school for all those who are outside educational establishments).

Web for Schools Project
http://wfs.eun.org

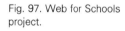
Fig. 97. Web for Schools project.

This is a project involving over 700 teachers in 150 schools. These schools are involved in a large number of school projects, which

range right across the curriculum. The projects are known as *timeline projects* because they develop and change over space and time. The *helpdesk* sections are particularly useful to new users with advice on web-authoring, pedagogic matters relating to internet use in schools and training materials, some of which are in a PowerPoint-style format. Web for Schools also produces a magazine called *Context*. A recent issue was circulated with an Internet Starter Kit CD-ROM that explains the potential of the internet.

Fig. 98. Eduweb for schools.

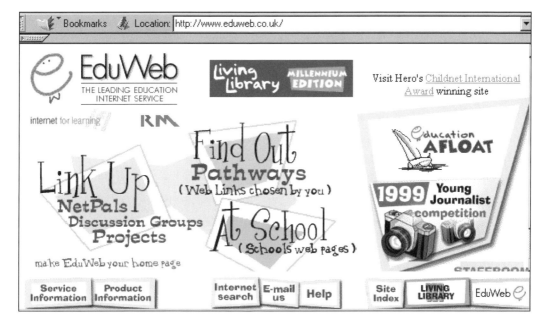

Web sites for schools ....

CHAPTER 2

Getting connected is not difficult
(mainly internet providers)

BT Internet
http://www.bt.net
BT's main internet service for home users. The company has also launched BTClick (September 1998) which does not involve a monthly payment. Subscribers are charged by usage.

LineOne
http://www.lineone.co.uk
BT's Online Service with content from News International (publisher of the *Sun* and *The Times*).

Demon
http://www.demon.net
Demon Internet, one of the largest and first UK providers. Now owned by Scottish Telecom.

AOL
http://www.aol.com
America Online – the largest UK online service provider.

VirginNet
http://www.virgin.net
Virgin's site has some good educational links. Virgin became a free service from 1 April 1999.

Pipex
http://www.uunet.pipex.com
UUNet Pipex (Dial) site – expensive but reliable internet service provider.

Microsoft
http://www.msn.com
Microsoft's Internet Provider site.

EduWeb
http://www.eduweb.co.uk
Research Machines as an internet service provider. Excellent links from this home page plus staff room discussion areas and advice on designing web pages.

Edex
http://www.edex.co.uk
Another excellent educational UK internet service provider. Edex offers some good deals to connect up school networks to the internet.

Enterprise

http://www.enterprise.net
Medium size internet service provider. Offers free accounts to schools.

Freeserve

www.freeserve.co.uk
Launched late September 1998. Could revolutionise the world of internet service providers. Offers free access to the internet. Financed by Dixons.

Tesconet

www.tesco.net
Free service to Clubcard holders. Tesco is also involved in an ambitious millennium project.

Fig. 99. Freeserve internet access.

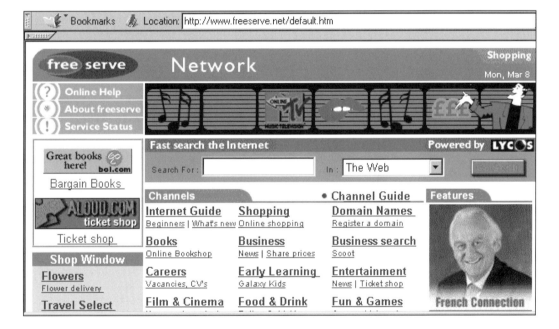

Web sites for schools ....

CHAPTER 3

Making contact by email

Bigfoot

http://www.bigfoot.co.uk

The place to find email addresses with a powerful search engine. Also offers free email accounts and web space.

Epals

http://epals.com

This site boasts over 6,000 classrooms from 70 countries (and 60 different languages) involved with email projects. Founded in 1996, over 150,000 students and teachers from 6,000 schools have registered. There is a search engine for the database of registered institutions. The teacher-monitored projects deal with a large number of areas including languages, arts, geography and social science as well as penpal links. In the future this organisation hopes to move into voice and video communication over the internet. All you have to do is submit a classroom profile to get started.

Eudora

http://www.qualcomm.com

Here is the place to pick up free or paid versions of Eudora, one of the main email clients. Eudora Lite is free and is postcard-ware. If you adopt it, just send an interesting postcard to the programmer. Manuals for Eudora, in Word format, are also available here.

ExcitePost

http://www.excitepost.co.uk

This site offers safe web-based email accounts to UK students. Students can only mail to addresses in their address book. Excite patrols messages held on their server.

Hilites

http://archives.gsn.org/hilites/

A service of the Global SchoolNet Foundation. An excellent source for email projects. Search the archives at the above URL to survey previous projects. There is a mailing list that alerts you to new proposals for collaborative email ventures. Details of these projects appear regularly in the uk-schools mailing list (see Chapter 5).

NetPals

http://www.rmplc.co.uk/netpals.htm

One of several places to find key-pals on the internet. It caters for anyone between the ages of 5 and 19 looking to write using email. A search engine is provided to produce suitable matches. There are useful tips on how to find the right people and how to stay safe online. Students are advised to withhold their last name, address and telephone number and only to meet NetPals in the company of adults.

Tucows

http://www.tucows.com

A very good site for internet shareware. Contains reviews on many categories of web utilities. Programs are ranked by a cow star system!

Turnpike

http://www.turnpike.co.uk

Site for the Turnpike suite of internet utilities. Now owned by Demon internet. An excellent set of programs, though internet Explorer and Windows98 contain most of them for free! (Well, yes, you need to pay for these if you have an old computer.)

Web66

http://web66.coled.umn.edu/

A great site! Named after the famous old highway Route 66 from Chicago to Los Angeles, a road forever going somewhere. The site aims to:

help educationalists set up their own internet servers
help them link servers
provide them with appropriate resources on the web
provide pointers to them.

The site has the following features:

▷ lists of school servers

▷ resources to help teachers surf the net efficiently

▷ information about web utilities – browsers etc.

▷ locations of educational mailing lists and a discussion group for webmasters.

All this is provided by the University of Minnesota.

Web sites for schools ....

CHAPTER 4

Usenet – a very useful resource

CIX
http://www.cix.co.uk
UK organisation that hosts a large number of discussion groups for its subscribers. Also provides an internet connection. Charges by the time online.

Dejanews
http://www.dejanews.com
One of the best search engines for usenet newsgroups. The site also contains links to the latest new stories and there is a directory to major topics on the web. This is an excellent place to search for information on a whole range of educational topics across the educational news-groups. It is also a good place to find groups that you did not know existed.

Free Agent
http://www.forteinc.com
Free Agent news and mail reading program is available here along with various new Forte products.

Reference.com
http://www.reference.com
Similar site to Dejanews. It claims that it makes it easy to find, browse, search and participate in more than 150,000 newsgroups, mailing lists and web forums through a powerful search engine. Contains guides to:

▷ how to find forums and lists
▷ how to participate in them.

Supernews
http://www.supernews.com
Another site that allows you to find previous postings in usenet.

CHAPTER 5

Want some mail? Join a mailing list!

Listbot
http://www.listbot.com
This site will allow you to set up your own discussion list for free. The catch is that each mailing will carry an advert in the near future. There are plenty of FAQs to get you going. A good place to start an educational mailing list between teachers with a particular curricular interest.

Liszt
http://www.liszt.com
Liszt's search engine will find most publicly available lists for you.

L-soft
http://www.lsoft.com
Producers of Listserv and other utilities.

Mailbase
http://www.mailbase.ac.uk
Mailbase – educational UK mailing lists site. You find here the archives of uk-schools, the main UK educational list, plus, of course, many others.

Oneline
http://www.oneline.com
Start your own mailing list here. Similar service to Listbot.

Public Accessible Mailing Lists
http://www.neosoft.com/internet/paml
Another list searching engine.

Reference.com
http://www.reference.com
Search thousands of mailing lists, usenet and web forums.

Web sites for schools ....

CHAPTER 6

Explore the world wide web from your armchair

General search engines

Hotbot
http://www.hotbot.com
Wired magazine's engine. Good for finding people's names on sites. Search results are produced a 100 at a time. There is also a *Wired* daily newsletter that can be emailed to your mailbox.

Northern Light
http://www.northernlight.com
Try this one! Often succeeds where others fail. Charges are made for specialist searches.

Excite
http://www.excite.co.uk
UK version of Excite. Comes with a reasonable site directory. Its large database is frequently updated.

Infoseek
http://www.infoseek.co.uk
UK version of Infoseek. Easy to search and fast but smaller database than AltaVista.

Yahoo!
http://www.yahoo.co.uk
Premier directory – large and easy to navigate by subject. Offers specialist services such as weather reports, *yellow pages* and sports news. Available in several major world languages. Can be configured to your own design.

AltaVista
http://www.altavista.com
Premier search engine. Huge, speedy and provides a translation service into several languages. Offers AV Family Filter that reduces the chance that objectionable material is viewed in the course of a search. Also boasts spell-checking and translation facilities!

Lycos
http://www.lycos.co.uk
Lycos' UK site. Smaller database than AltaVista but allows highly discriminate web searches.

Webcrawler
http://www.webcrawler.co.uk
Webcrawler's search engine. Smaller than AltaVista or Excite.

Looksmart
http://www.looksmart.com
Linked with AltaVista. Every result includes a comment.

Search engines for parents, families and children

Ask Jeeves for kids
http://www.ajkids.com
Allows searches that are couched in everyday English.

Dig
http://www.disney.com/dig/today
Disney's kids' site.

Personal Lycos
http://personal.lycos.com/safetynet/safetynet.asp
Lycos site that allows the blocking of unsuitable addresses.

Yahooligans!
http://www.yahooligans.com
Yahoo!'s kids' site.

Family orientated search engines

RCLS
http://www.rcls.org/ksearch.htm
Search engines for families

Fig. 100. Yahooligans!
for kids.

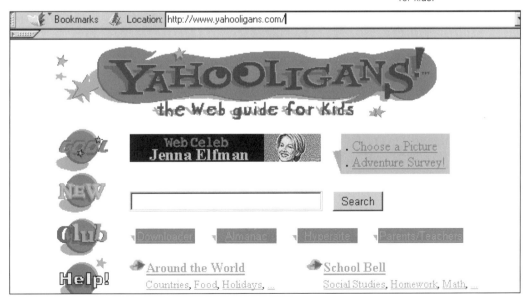

Web sites for schools ....

Meta search tools etc

MetaCrawler
http://www.metacrawler.com
Search site. Provides search results from a number of search engines.
Try also Mamma at www.mamma.com.

Savvy Search
http://www.savvysearch.com
Savvy Search has come out of its experimental stage.

Ask Jeeves
http://www.askjeeves.com
Ask Jeeves for help! Allows searches in sentence format.

Electronic Yellow Pages
http://www.yell.co.uk
Internet equivalent of the *Yellow Pages* printed directory. Good for travel information.

Four11
http://www.four11.com
Email address search program

Utilities – cache readers and players

Secret Agent
http://www.ariel.co.uk
Secret Agent cache reader. Suitable for Netscape and internet Explorer. Useful for building intranet pages.

Unmozify
http://www.evolve.co.uk
Another cache reader.

RealPlayer
http://www.real.com
RealPlayer5 is found on many magazine disks. Allows you to play sound and video files.

Other useful web sites for teachers

Association for Science
http://www.ase.org.uk/webschl.html
Teachers helping teachers to teach science. Excellent source of information for science teachers. There is a particularly good links page to science-biased sites including favourites Web66 and Netpals. The *Science across the World* site involves teachers and businesses in 36 countries.

Electronic Telegraph

http://www.telegraph.co.uk/

One of the first and still one of the best online newspapers. The site carries an abbreviated version of the newspaper. You need to register to access the site but there are no charges; advertisers pay for the maintenance of the site. Good source for the teaching of IT.

Luminarium

http://www.luminarium.org

Award-winning site with information and resources on medieval, Renaissance and seventeenth-century English literature. Complete texts can be downloaded.

Microsoft Europe

http://www.eu.microsoft.com/

This is the European site for Microsoft and is usually easier to access than the US one. It is a good place to find technical briefings and information on software upgrades. There is also a series of free email newsletters including a good one for FrontPage. A good place to enquire about technical fixes.

The Met Office

http://www.meto.govt.uk

The UK National Weather Service site. Carries information on the work of the Meteorological Office, forecasts, UK satellite images, links to other weather sites and information on how weather is forecast.

NASA

http://www.nasa.gov/

Contains links to many space-related resources. There is a library of photographs, news stories and pictures from the Hubble Space Telescope. Science teachers will find lesson plans and resources here.

STEM Project

http://www.nmsi.ac.uk/education/stem/

The aim of the STEM (Students' and Teachers' Educational Materials) is to encourage the development and sharing, though the web, of educational resources relating to the National Museum of Science and Industry (this consists of the London Science Museum, the National Railway Museum in York and the National Museum of Photography, Film and Television in Bradford). Materials signposted on the site can be downloaded and adapted to suit the individual school's and teacher's own particular approach to teaching.

The Times Educational Supplement

http://www.tes.co.uk

Contains articles from the latest edition, a database of previous articles, and job adverts. You can even receive an email message about vacancies! Essential for all practising teachers.

Web sites for schools ....

Roger Frost's Science Site
http://www.rogerfrost.com
Excellent site for science teachers. Roger Frost has written extensively on IT and science education.

Spartacus History Site
htttp://www.spartacus.schoolnet.co.uk
John Simpson's wonderful history site will hook many history teachers to the web.

Right: Roger Frost's science site. *Below:* part of the Spartacus history site, a page with many links to the history of education.

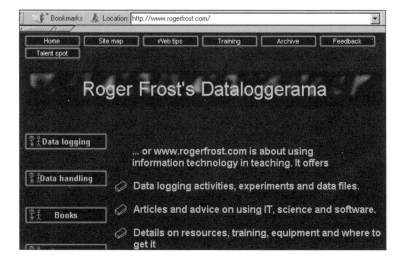

CHAPTER 7

Play safe on the internet

Smartparent
http://smartparent.com
The aim of this site is to educate parents on the best way to safeguard
children from the dangers of cyberspace. It contains information on:

▷ blocking and filtering software
▷ protection tips
▷ parent and child-friendly sites.

There is even a Smartparent newsletter! You'll also find links to
organisations and agencies that focus on internet-related issues. There
is also a latest news section (on developments in child-safe use of the
internet).

Parents' Information Network
http://www.pin-parents.com
The network publishes a range of free leaflets for parents. These
include advice on buying computers and safe internet access.

RASC homepage
http://www.rasc.org/homepage.asp
US organisation that is pioneering a ratings system for child-safe sites.

Internetwatch
http://www.internetwatch.co.uk
European site concerned with self-regulation of the web.

National Center for Missing and Exploited Children.
http://www.ncmec.org/
Contains much sound advice for family safe use of the internet.

Net Nanny
http://www.netnanny.com
Filtering software for home use, like the following three sites:

Cyber Patrol
http://www.cyberpatrol.com

Cybersitter
http://www.solidoak.com/cysitter.htm
(see Figure 101).

Surfwatch
http://www.surfwatch.com

Web sites for schools ....

Fig. 101. Cybersitter filtering.

Cybertimer
http://www.solidoak.com/cytimer.htm
Solidoak's timing program. Allows you to restrict student access to certain time slots.

Watchdog
http://www.sarna.net/watchdog/
No connection with the BBC consumer television programme!
Site for Watchdog filtering program.

Time's Up
http://www.timesup.com
Package that offers filtering and time restrictions in one.

Wingate
http://www.wingate.net
Site for Wingate Pro. Allows network users to monitor sites accessed by students where Wingate is used as a proxy server.

WebRanger
http://www.rangersuite.co.uk
Download an evaluation copy of the WebRanger program that allows monitoring of student and staff use of the web.

CHAPTERS 8 AND 9

Web site creation

Microsoft Frontpage
http://www.microsoft.com/frontpage/
The Microsoft FrontPage product support page offers a wealth of information on those who use their product to design web sites. Not only are you given details of internet service providers who support the FrontPage server extensions, but you can also download extra themes to use.

Web Pages for absolute beginners
http://subnet.virtual-pc.com/li542871/index.html
As the site suggests it is aimed at those with absolutely minimal knowledge of web pages design. Although this site looks really simple, it has the advantage of being fast to download and very well organised, making navigation for novices easy. A grounding in HTML is given first, which may not suit everyone, but the site is an interesting start on your journey to page creation.

The Site Creator
http://www.btinternet.com/~mike.bednarek/sitecreator/index.htm
A very comprehensive site that covers every aspect of web site creation, from the design stages through to launching and advertising. Written in plain English, the Site Creator is easy to navigate and fast to access, making it much less of a task to find the information you're looking for. Most sections include references, so that further information is just a mouse-click away.

The Mechanical Monkey
http://dspace.dial.pipex.com/leuhusen/index.shtml
A great site to visit for the layout alone. The Mechanical Monkey offers comprehensive advice on HTML, Java, Mail and graphics, including downloadable software such as an HTML editor to do the work for you. Well worth a visit is the graphics section, which includes some excellent images you can use for your own home page or school web site. To do this, right-click on the image and choose 'Save picture as'. Then browse to the location where you want it to save to.

The Pixel Pen
http://home.earthlink.net/~thomasareed/pixelpen/
Another page dedicated to the absolute beginner in page authoring, the Pixel Pen couldn't be simpler to use. Designed to look like a book, it offers clear advice and information on what your site should contain and how to put it there. The checklist is a great feature, to make sure that you haven't missed anything when completing your site.

Web sites for schools ....

WebHome Improvement
http://www.htmltips.com/
Advertised as a 'Web design style guide', this site is great. If you get sick of all of the techies going on about HTML and want to use a WYSIWIG editor to create your page, visit this site. It discusses the good and bad points of site design and creation in a plain but informative way. Highly recommended.

Web Design Tips
http://www.colin.mackenzie.org/webdesign/
What makes this site so good is that it is short and sweet. Many pages contain page upon page of text. Busy teachers often don't have the time (or inclination!) to sift through this to get the snippet they need. Less is often best.

Geocities Free Web Space
http://www.geocities.com/join/
Many companies offer free web space (and some even give you access to web design 'wizards'.) Geocities is one of the most popular. Once you've registered, you will be able to design a site with most of the features of a web site. As it's free, you may receive the occasional Spam email from Geocities, but that's a small price to pay for free web space!

The Clipart Directory
http://www.clipart.com/
Contains links to hundreds of sites that contain clipart and other graphics for you to incorporate into your home page or web site. Try browsing through some of these sites and saving any images that you think you could use. Read the Mechanical Monkey site review to see how to do this.

CUSAGC Guide and Scout Clipart Collection
http://spot.newhall.cam.ac.uk/cusagc/clipart/
A huge directory with over 2,500 images available to download. This site is not only comprehensive, but sensibly organised too. The images are listed according to category, making them much easier to find. Example categories include camping, animals, flags, people and religious. Because the Scouts and Guides create the site, you can be assured that the content is fine for children.

The Groan Zone
http://groan-zone.net/
A nice site dedicated to the distribution of free images for use on your site. The Zone is attractively presented and slick, making it easy to navigate to find the right images. I listed the page because it also contains downloadable resources to use within your web page when you become more confident at site creation. Bookmark the site for future reference.

Clipart Review
http://www.webplaces.com/html/clipart.htm
A magazine that reviews many sites offering free clipart and web images. Reading them before a visit can save you a great deal of time, which could otherwise have been wasted looking in the wrong place. This site got listed because it is organised by categories, and there are dozens of them! Example categories include Animals, Bells, Cemetery (!), Houses, internet, Trains and Weddings. If you're looking for that specific image to finish off your site, you'll find a site with it here!

Yahoo! 'suggest a site'
http://www.yahoo.com/info/suggest/
Once your page or site is finished it will need registering with the search engines and directories via the world wide web. Yahoo! is one of the most popular directories so it would be wise to register with them here. Although the process may seem lengthy (it will take you 20 minutes or so to fill out the forms) it is absolutely vital to do it. If you don't, nobody will know about your site!

Infoseek 'add URL'
http://www.infoseek.com/AddUrl?pg=DCaddurl.html
Register your site with the Infoseek search engine here. Be aware, though, that whereas Yahoo! page registration is available 24 hours a day, Infoseek periodically take their servers offline for maintenance. You may end up having to register at three in the morning!

Lycos 'add a site'
http://www.lycos.co.uk/search/addasite.html
Probably the least time-consuming of the site registration pages, Lycos like to keep it simple. This one will take you about two minutes. Your site will be spidered and added to their database within seven days. The advantage is that Lycos run the search technology for *Freeserve*, the new free UK internet service provider. With many schools taking up accounts with them, your educational site stands more chance of reaching the intended target audience.

AltaVista 'add a page'
http://www.altavista.com/av/content/addurl.htm
My favourite site registration page. AltaVista contains lots of information if you're new to page registration, including the use of meta-tags to describe your site content. What's more, it's fast (added to the index in less than a day) and attractively designed too. The page contains information on how to inform AltaVista that your site no longer exists at that address, vital to prevent others from wasting their time.

HotBot 'add URL'
http://www.hotbot.com/addurl.asp
The more engines you register with, the more you increase your hit-rate. Registration here is fast, and gives you the chance of subscribing to a free webzine that gives relevant news on the internet and world wide web.

Web sites for schools ....

Fig. 102. AltaVista
searches.

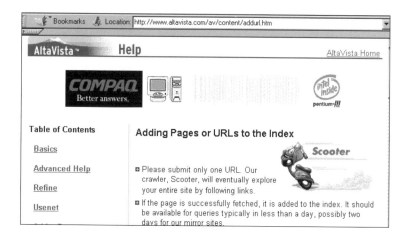

WebCrawler 'add my URL'

http://www.webcrawler.com/Help/GetListed/AddURLS.html

Finally another form to fill in and register the URL of your site. After that it's just a case of sitting back and watching the hits come in.

EduWeb Link Up

http://www.eduweb.co.uk/atschool/atschool.html

Research Machines PLC contain a large database of school web sites, along with tips on how to create your own. They will even give you some space upon which to publish your site. Now there really are no excuses!

CHAPTER 10

Transferring files across the globe

Explore the internet – Guide to FTP

http://www.ou.edu/research/electron/internet/zen-3.htm
Frequently Asked Questions about File Transfer Protocol (or FAQ about FTP!). Although the background to this site is orange, it does contain lots of useful information about FTP, including etiquette, connection and uses. I'd recommend cutting out the text and pasting it into a word processor though, as it may give you a headache!

The internet Helpdesk

http://w3.one.net/~alward/ntable.html
Another guide aimed at novices to the internet, the guide offers information and advice on everything internet. The URL above refers to the Troubleshooting Telnet/FTP Chart, a great resource if you're experiencing difficulties carrying out or setting up an FTP session. The chart has problems experienced on the left, along with possible solutions in the middle, and links to 'Tools and Tips' on the right.

Ipswitch Software – WS_FTP

http://www.ipswitch.com/
As the producers of WS_FTP, the Ipswitch Software site offers links to a downloadable evaluation version of the product. Of particular use are the software manuals, viewed in Adobe Acrobat Reader, which can provide extra help on the product beyond the electronic help facility. Also worth knowing is that you can email Ipswitch direct for help solving problems you may be having with your registered version of WS_FTP.

CuteFTP Web Site

http://www.cuteftp.com/
Again, follow the download links to get the software. It is nice to see the company offer a brief explanation of what FTP actually is! Good for beginners is the 'troubleshooting' section that can help diagnose and solve problems. If that fails, email the company to get a solution. These help facilities are even available for users still trialling the software.

FTPVoyager Web Site

http://www.ftpvoyager.com
A veritable celebration of how good FTPVoyager is, with reviews, awards and comparisons to sell you the product. Also in there somewhere is the evaluation version of the software along with unlimited email support for all users.

Usenet FTP archive

ftp://ftp.uu.net/usenet/news.answers/ftp-list/sitelist/
Usenet newsgroups are a great way for people to solve problems. Some kind soul has put together the most frequently asked questions into a zip file, which you can then download onto your computer to

browse at your leisure. If your problems really are serious enough, it is good to know the answer is out there!

Download.com

http://www.download.com/

If you'd rather not pay for your FTP software, choose a freeware version instead. Follow the links of internet FTP to get a list of available titles. Ensure it is a freeware version you download though! This software archive also contains some good educational shareware and even freeware for you to download and trial. Follow the appropriate links from the address given above. Alternatively find a search engine and try a keyword search.

Fig. 103. Download.

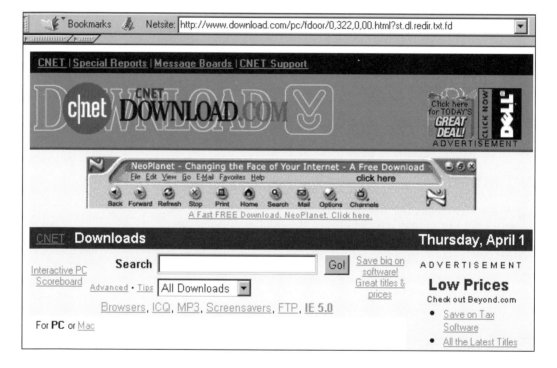

CHAPTER 11

Launching your school intranet

Netscape Virtual Intranet
http://home.netscape.com/comprod/at_work/vip/index.html
There are several 'virtual' intranets available online for you to explore and although the one by Netscape is targeted towards companies, it does give a good idea of what is possible when using an intranet.

Red Traktor Demo Intranet
www.redtraktor.com
Another good demo site, Red Traktor have made their site as simple as possible, using a minimum of images, incorporating mainly text hyperlinks. This minimises the need for expensive training.

Intranet Myths
http://www.intrack.com/intranet/intmyth10.shtml
10 myths about intranets that really must be read before you embark on an intranet project. Remember that a successful intranet within a school is an intranet that is used frequently and updated regularly.

Microsoft Intranet
http://www.microsoft.com/office/intranet/
Everything you could ever want to know about intranets (but were afraid to ask!). The site offers advice on building a site (in less than half an hour), how to design your intranet, a guided tour of an intranet published using FrontPage98 and so on. Microsoft also allow you to download a zipped-up intranet template for use with FrontPage98. Well worth a visit.

Fig. 104. Microsoft Intranet.

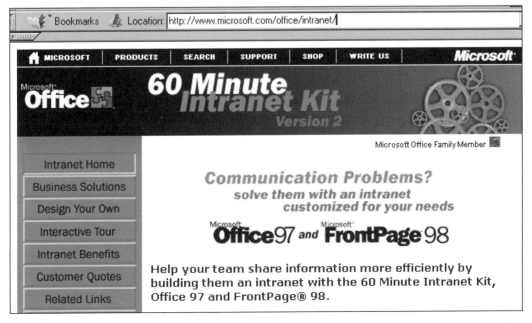

Web sites for schools ···

CHAPTER 12

A glimpse of the future

The first five sites here are also reviewed in Chapter 1.

The National Grid for Learning

http://www.ngfl.gov.uk

The home page of the Grid, which is currently moving from the prototype stages to the fully working resource. Many of the resources and links in the four rooms are being updated at present, so regular visits to this site is an absolute must. Hopefully the Grid will eventually contain lots of references to sites that contain educational resources to help you teach.

BECTA

http://www.becta.org

The British Education Communications Technology Agency site has a fantastic range of resources for teachers of all levels and subjects, including practical ideas about how to use the internet as a teaching resource.

BBC Education

http://www.bbc.co.uk/education

The BBC education site contains a wealth of useful materials to help students and teachers within the classroom. The site is made up of 3 main sections – 'Today's Choice', with educational information about the day's programming, BBC Schools Online and the BBC Learning Zone. Schools Online is designed for parents, children and teachers, and is a 'must see' site for anyone who wants to learn more about the internet and education.

BBC Webguide

http://db.bbc.co.uk/education-webguide/pkg_main.p_home

Part of the BBC Education site, the Webguide offers reviews of sites that contain subject-specific content. So, for example, a student or teacher could search for content to suit their needs, like primary geography.

Channel 4 Schools

http://schools.channel4.com/home_002.cfm

Looking for a maths television programme for your Year Tens on algebra? This site contains a great search tool that lets you find out if Channel 4 is broadcasting one. This saves time, and ensures you don't miss the broadcast. For any programmes that you find you can see a transcript of the content. The Net Notes resource breaks down each programme into aims, relevance to the National Curriculum and so on, making the site a fantastic resource.

Gridlink Online Education System
http://www.rmplc.co.uk/eduweb/sites/ctrh/home.htm
An example of a British company who specialise in offering distance learning to out-of-school students. The site includes details of what kinds of course are offered, examples of distance-learning events and work portfolios completed by students who have taken part.

Distance Learning Over the Net
http://www.hoyle.com/distance.htm
An informative site which begins with a definition of distance education, as well as including references to schools who have begun distance learning initiatives with their students. Although the site is based on the USA, the content is extremely useful nonetheless. Written by Glenn Hoyle.

How to offer a course on the internet
http://www.edgorg.com/course.htm
A simple and easy-to-follow site which details preparation prior to setting up the course, the course itself and a recommended teaching approach. All useful material which will provide you with baseline knowledge from which to explore the other resources available.

Distance Education at a Glance
http://www.uidaho.edu/evo/distglan.html
A series of 14 guides, each of which covers an aspect of distance learning. Visiting this site really is a must for those wishing to set up a distance-learning scheme within a school. Be warned, though, it will take you some time to digest it all! I recommend you cut and paste the guides into a word-processor and then print them out.

Ibid Whiteboards
http://www.microtouch.com/ibid/
Although a US company, the site gives quite a lot of information on the capabilities whiteboards can offer, along with the technical specification to look out for.

Teamboard Whiteboards
http://www.teamboard.com/
Another company gives details on the latest whiteboard technology available. Try the tour, using the buttons at the bottom of the screen.

Access provider
An **internet service provider**, or **online service provider**.

ActiveX controls
Multimedia programming system developed by Microsoft that extends the capabilities of web browsers.

Alias
A type of nickname allowed by email clients so that 'Fred' is really fsmith@aol.com.

Animated GIF
A type of **GIF** image that can be animated by combining several images into a single **GIF** file. Applications that support the animated **GIF** standard, GIF89A, cycle through each image. GIF animation doesn't give the same level of control or flexibility as other animation formats but it has become extremely popular because nearly all browsers support it. In addition, animated GIF files tend to be quite a bit smaller than other animation files, such as **Java** applets.

ARPANET/DARPANET
Forerunner of the internet developed by US military and universities.

Article
Term for a message posted to a newsgroup. The message may only be a few words.

Attachment
A file sent with an email message. It can consist of a word-processed document, graphic file, spreadsheet, sound file, or any other kind of file.

AUP
Acceptable use policy – a policy statement to be read and agreed to by all users of the internet or computer systems in an institution.

Bandwidth
The size of the data 'pipe'. The wider the 'pipe'

the quicker the data flows.

Banner
Usually situated at the top of a web page, a banner acts like a title, telling the user what the content of the page is about.

Binary files (binaries)
A non-text file. Can include programs, graphics and sound files.

Bit
Stands for binary digit, in other words 0 or 1. Characters (for instance letters and numbers) on PCs are usually represented by 8 bits which is one byte. The speed at which data is transmitted across a network is often measured in bits per second.

Bookmarks
A list of web sites you visit frequently, or want to remember. If you are online and click on 'bookmarks', your Netscape browser will open up the relevant web page. You can add bookmarks while you are surfing. If you use Internet Explorer the term is **favorites**.

Boolean
A type of search involving 'operators' – words such as AND, OR or EITHER OR. It is named after George Boole, nineteenth-century English mathematician.

Bounced email
Email returned to sender because it was unable to reach its destination.

Browse
To explore, or look for or view a file, web page or directory.

Browser
Software originally written so that people could browse web pages. The modern browser can handle most of your internet needs including email and newsreading. The two best known browsers are Netscape and Internet Explorer.

Glossary

Bulletin board
A bulletin board system (BBS) is a computer service that provides an email service and file archive. It is not usually part of the internet. The internet equivalent is usenet (newsgroups).

Cache
A temporary storage area usually on your hard disk that allows a web browser to store pages that have been recently opened. It allows the browser to quickly load these pages if you decide to return to them.

CampusWorld
British Telecom's educational service (see the Appendix for the URL). See also **walled garden** and **filtered service**.

Chat
Real-time communication between two or more people using computers. Once chat has been initiated, either user can enter text by typing on the keyboard and the entered text will appear on the other user's monitor. In order to participate in chat a user will need a network or internet connection and the appropriate software. Commonly used examples are MIRC and Microsoft Chat.

Client
A computer program, such as email or news, which makes use of its counterpart, a **server**. Hence the terms *client-side* and *server-side*.

Cookie
A very small text file placed on your hard disk (with your permission) by a web page server. It is uniquely yours and can only be read by the server that gave it to you. Its purpose is to tell the server when you have returned to that web page.

Cross posting
Usually refers to **usenet** and involves posting the same message to several newsgroups. This is not popular if carried out indiscriminately.

Data protection
Government legislation protecting the rights of data subjects, i.e. you.

Default
A standard value or name that the computer gives to a changeable piece of information, such as a filename.

Dial up
Accessing the internet via a standard telephone line. It therefore does not involve a permanent connection.

Directory
A defined storage area for files on a computer disk. From Windows95 onwards, directories have been known as 'folders'.

DNS
A Domain Name Server. This translates a human-friendly domain name into an unfriendly **IP address** consisting of a row of digits.

Domain name
A name that identifies a computer on the internet. For example in the URL 'www.internetforschools.co.uk' the domain name is 'internetforschools'. See **DNS**.

Download
To collect data from a remote computer (someone else's computer) to a local computer (your own computer).

Email
Short for electronic mail. If you have an email account, your will have a unique email address. This will have an 'at' sign in the middle, like this: anyuser@host

Emoticons
Symbols which have popularly evolved to express emotions in email, for example:

:-) = Smiling!

Emoticons are not normally appropriate in business or professional communications, any more than they would be in equivalent correspondence.

Encryption
The process of scrambling a message so that a key, held only by authorised recipients, is needed to unscramble and read the message. Most commonly applies to email

although with the advent of purchasing online, encryption is being used to secure payments for goods purchased in this way.

Extranet

An intranet which is accessible from a remote location, usually via a direct dial-up connection to the host web server.

FAQ

Frequently Asked Questions. Answers to these are found in most usenet newsgroups, and increasingly on web sites.

Favorites

A list of web sites you visit frequently, or want to remember. If you are online and click on a 'favorite', your browser will open up the relevant web page. You can add favorites while you are surfing. The term is used in Internet Explorer and AOL. If you use a Netscape browser, the term is **bookmark**.

File transfer protocol (FTP)

A simple means of transferring files between computers linked to the internet. See **protocol**.

Filtered service

An internet service which blocks access to sites deemed inappropriate for children or indeed other user groups.

Flaming

Popular term for sending an unpleasant/ negative message to an internet newsgroup or mailing list.

Folder

A directory in which files are stored on a computer. The term 'folder' has replaced the term 'directory' since the advent of Windows 95.

Form

A method of data collection on web pages. The on-screen form uses text boxes and buttons. Many cheap web-authoring packages such as Microsoft FrontPage include the facility to create online forms.

Frames

A feature which allows web pages to be divided up into discrete areas, each of which usually contains separate information. A typical set of frames includes an index frame, header frame, and body frame.

Freeware

Computer software which is available free, often by downloading it from the internet. *See also* **shareware**.

Gateway site

Popular term for a web site containing hundreds of links to sites of related interest. There are many educational gateway sites of interest to UK teachers. Another word meaning the same thing is 'portal'.

GIF

Pronounced *jiff* or *giff* (hard g), stands for graphics interchange format, a bitmapped graphics file format used on the world wide web. GIF supports colour and various resolutions. It also includes data compression making it especially effective for scanned photographs. Only used for images with less than 256 colours.

Gopher

A system of cataloguing mainly text materials on the internet, before the web became popular. The gopher system is still available on some university sites.

History list

When you are browsing the web, your browser keeps a list or 'history' of all the web pages you visit. You can inspect this list in your browser, and delete some or all of the listings if you wish.

Home page

A world wide web document which is usually made up of a single page. Hyperlinks on the page can be mouse-clicked to view related pages, send mail, download a file, or jump to external sites.

HTML

Hypertext mark up language – a special scripting language used to write web pages. It is a kind of word processing that uses a

Glossary

variety of 'tags' to format the material.

HTTP

A **protocol** that allows hypermedia links to be made across the internet. Every world wide web address begins with the characters http://

Hyper link

The links within one document that allows it to connect to and display another document. Selecting a hypertext link automatically displays the second document. Text hyperlinks are commonly displayed underlined to indicate their function. Images may also act as hyper links, as in the case of buttons.

Hyper text

A special way of storing information, invented by Ted Nelson in the 1960s, in which objects (text, pictures, music, programs etc) can be creatively linked to each other. When you select an object (usually by clicking on it with the mouse pointer) you can see all of the other objects that are linked to it. Hyper text systems are particularly useful for browsing through large collections of information that contain different types of information. Hyper text is the central concept behind navigating the world wide web.

IfL

Internet for Learning, Research Machines' internet service (see the Appendix for its URL). See also **walled garden** and **filtered service**.

Index page

The first page encountered when visiting a web site. It is also known as the welcome page, title page, or first page.

Internet

A broad term which refers to the global network of all computers linked together via their internet service providers. Its main components are the world wide web, usenet (newsgroups), and email.

Internet relay chat (IRC)

A mechanism that allows for a number of internet users to connect to the same network and chat in real time. To access this feature,

you need to access an IRC server and the appropriate software, such as MIRC which you can download from:

www.mirc.com

A typical IRC chat session will involve a number of people all 'chatting' about a certain topic. Like all features of the internet a set of 'rules' and standards have evolved regarding behaviour within these chat environments (see **Netiquette**). Similarly a number of acronyms are commonly used. Here are some IRC-unique communication shortcuts:

AAMOF	As a matter of fact.
BBFN	Bye bye for now.
BTW	Back to work.
BYKT	But you know that.
CMIIW	Correct me if I'm wrong.
EOL	End of lecture.
FITB	Fill in the blank.
IAC	In any case.
IMHO	In my humble opinion.
LJBF	Let's just be friends.
LOL	Laugh out loud.
OIC	Oh, I see.
OTOH	On the other hand.
ROFL	Rolling on the floor laughing.
TIC	Tongue in cheek.
TTFN	Ta ta for now.
TYVM	Thank you very much.
<G>	Grinning.
<S>	Smiling.
<L>	Laughing.
<J>	Joking.

Internet service provider (ISP)

A company that provides access to the internet, usually for a fee.

Intranet

A private network that uses internet standards and protocols to facilitate communication between individuals. It often operates on a **local area network** (LAN).

IP address

Internet protocol address. All computers on the internet have an IP address. It consists of four numbers separated by dots. It somewhat resembles a telephone number.

ISDN
Integrated Services Digital Network – a high speed communications standard that allows a telephone line to carry digital and voice data.

ISP
See **internet service provider**.

Java
A high-level programming language developed by Sun Microsystems. Java was originally called OAK and was designed for hand held devices and set-top boxes. OAK was unsuccessful so in 1995 Sun changed the name to Java and modified the language to take advantage of the world wide web. Similar to C++, Java source code files are compiled into a format called byte code which can then be run by a program called a Java interpreter. Such compiled Java code can be run on most computers because Java interpreters exist for most machines. This compatibility makes Java well suited to the world wide web. Small Java programs called applets can be incorporated into web pages to make the pages more dynamic and attractive to the user. However in order to run these applets the user must have a Java-compatible browser such as Netscape Navigator or Microsoft Internet Explorer.

JavaScript
A language designed by Netscape to enable web page authors to design interactive sites. Although it shares many features with the full version of Java, it was developed independently. JavaScript is an open-source programming language which means that anyone can use it without purchasing a license. JavaScript is at the heart of a recent court case involving Microsoft.

JPEG
This is short for Joint Photographic Experts Group, and is pronounced *jay-peg*. JPEG is a compression technique for colour images. Although it can reduce files to about 5% of their normal size, some detail is lost in the compression. Compressing the size of the file makes the time it takes a user to download much shorter therefore speeding up the process of viewing web pages.

Links
In hypertext systems and the world wide web, a link is a reference to another file, which can take the form of another web page, an image or sound.

Listserver
A robot computer that handles mailing lists.

Local area network (LAN)
This is a computer network usually found in one building.

Log on/log off
To access or leave a network. In the early days of computing this was recorded in a log book.

Lurking
Popular term for reading messages in a newsgroup, without taking part yourself by posting messages of your own. Lurking is a perfectly respectable activity.

Mail server
Remote server which has the primary job of handling email for a group of subscribers. Usually located at your access provider.

Main content
The bulk of the text on a web page which contains the information relating to that page.

Meta tool
A powerful search program that makes use of other search engines. An example is Metacrawler.

Minicomputer
More powerful than a micro and less powerful than a mainframe computer. It is often used for a specific purpose such as data-processing in a medium size company.

Mirror site
An exact replica of another web site, located somewhere else on the internet. Some big software suppliers for example have mirror sites in different parts of the world, so that customers can download their software products more quickly. People fearful of hostile action, such as dissidents, may put up mirror sites in case their main site is closed down by a hostile regime.

Glossary ....

Modem
An electronic device that allows remote computers to communicate with one another over an analogue telephone line. They can be internal (fitted inside the computer box) or external (plugged into the back). There are many brands on the market. An important factor is the modem's speed in transferring information to and from your computer.

Multimedia
The inclusion of more than one type of media in a program, for example text and sound.

National Grid for Learning
A UK government education initiative to upgrade information technology skills of the teaching profession through use of internet and computers generally.

Navigate
To navigate means mouse-clicking the hyperlinks on a web site in order to move ('jump') to other web locations.

Net
Shorthand term for the **internet**.

Netscape
The company which brought the first popular browser into use, Netscape Navigator. This has now evolved into Netscape Communicator, which contains a free web authoring tool Netscape Page Composer. In 1998 Netscape was taken over for billions of dollars by America Online. Netscape Communicator is widely available free on the glossy internet magazine CD Roms. Its great competitor is Microsoft's browser, Internet Explorer.

Netiquette
An informal code of rules which has evolved, which most people observe when writing email and posting to usenet newsgroups.

Network
Any system involving two or more computers being linked together directly, or by telephone or any other communication links.

Newbie
New member of a newsgroup or mailing list. A newbie should take care before sending a first posting to a newsgroup, or mailing to a mailing list.

News reader
Software package whose function is to interact with **usenet**. It allows you to subscribe to, read, reply to and unsubscribe from newsgroups.

News server
Remote computer that holds **usenet** data.

Newsgroup
A discussion group that forms part of **usenet**. There are upwards of 30,000 different newsgroups, each concerned with some specific interest or subject area.

Offline
In terms of the internet, to be offline is not to have an active connection.

Online
To have an active connection and to be able to use the various components of the internet.

Online service provider (OSP).
An internet provider that also offers its own content not generally available over the internet. This content could include its own news pages, member chat rooms, entertainment pages, and other features.

OSP
See **online service provider**.

Packet
A bundle of data. On the internet, data is broken into small chunks, called packets. Each packet travels across the network independently. Each packet contains details of its sender and destination and place in the complete file.

PGP
'Pretty Good Privacy' – state of the art software for strong encryption. It has been developed by an American mathematician who has made it freely available worldwide to support personal privacy and civil liberties. PGP is effectively uncrackable, and governments everywhere (including the UK)

are trying to bring in laws to stop people and organisations using it without handing over their 'keys' (passwords). It has become a major civil liberties issue in the USA, and is likely to become so in Europe.

Plug-in
In terms of the world wide web, a plug-in is software that is needed to add a special feature to a web browser. For example, there are plug-ins available for Netscape Navigator that enable it to play different types of audio or video messages. Without such plug-ins the user would not be able to access the files. Plug-ins are usually available to download free.

POP
Stands for point of presence, an access provider's range of local dial-in points. Demon, for instance, provides VPOPs – virtual pops which have local call telephone numbers.

Portal site
See **gateway**.

Post/posting
To send a message to a usenet newsgroup. Posting a message is very like sending an email.

Protocol
A set of rules that allows computers of different types to communicate.

PSTN
Public Switched Telephone Network – standard telephone line.

QuickTime
A video and animation system developed by Apple Computers. QuickTime format files can be run on PCs using a QuickTime driver. QuickTime is competing with a number of other standards, including AVI and ActiveMovie. In February 1998, the ISO standards body gave QuickTime a boost by deciding to use it as the basis for the new MPEG-4 standard it is defining.

RSACi
Rating system for web pages aimed at giving adults control over internet access for minors. RSACi stands for Recreational Software Advisory Council.

RealAudio
The de facto standard for sending audio data over the world wide web. RealAudio was developed by RealNetworks and supports FM-stereo-quality sound. To hear a web-page that includes a RealAudio file you will need to obtain a RealAudio player, (a piece of software that translates the file into sound), which is available free from www.real.com.

Refresh/reload
When browsing the web, you can make a web page download again by hitting the refresh or reload button in your browser. It's a good idea to do this if you are having trouble downloading the page, or if you want to make sure you are looking at the most recent version of the page (and not one stored in your **cache** from a previous viewing).

Search engine
A special program developed to search and make sense of the vast amount of information on the web. The search engine builds its own index of web pages.

SENCO
Special Educational Needs Coordinator – promoted teaching post holder responsible for supporting the education of students with individual needs.

Server
A computer that has the task of giving out ('serving') data to other computers.

Shareware
Computer software which is offered for a small charge, typically from $10 to $30. You can often try it out before sending payment.

Shockwave
A technology developed by Macromedia Inc. that enables web pages to include multimedia features. Shockwave allows pages to have sound, animation, video and even processes a user's mouse-clicks. In order to access web pages featuring Shockwave you will need to acquire the Shockwave **plug-in**, available

Glossary

form www.macromedia.com/shockwave.

Signature

Personal footer that can be automatically attached to email or usenet messages. Often consists of a witty or philosophical saying.

Smileys

See emoticons.

Source (code)

This refers to the hyper text mark up language used to create web pages. In addition to viewing an actual web page, your browser will also let you view the HTML source which has been written to create the page.

Spam

Popular term for unwanted multiple email or **usenet** postings. The term derives from a Monty Python sketch.

Stack

Technical term referring here to TCP/IP. Consists of the ordered series of protocols and packet drivers needed to interface a desktop computer with the internet.

Streaming

A technique for transferring data so that it can be processed as a steady continuous stream. For example, a user wanting to listen to a large audio file using the world wide web does not have to wait for all of the file to be downloaded before listening to it, but can begin listening as soon as the start of the file begins to arrive. Due to current bandwidth restrictions, streaming is limited to audio files, although with a good connection poor quality video can be streamed too. The *de facto* standard for streaming audio files is RealAudio format.

Subheading

On a web page subheadings divide up the main content.

Supercomputer

A computer with massive processing power; more powerful than a mainframe.

TCP/IP

Stands for Transmission Control Protocol/

Internet Protocol. This is an agreed set of computer communication rules and standards that allow communication between different types of computers and networks that are connected to the internet.

Telnet

Software that allows you to connect to a remote machine. It allows you to act as if you had your own terminal on that system.

Template

A partially completed web page that just needs slight alterations to become complete. For example a template page will allow you to add your own text and images.

Theme

In terms of the world wide web, a theme describes the general colours and graphics used within a web site. Many popular web authoring packages offer an assortment of readymade themes as templates, complete with matching backgrounds, buttons, rules and borders

Thread

An ongoing topic in a usenet newsgroup or mailing list discussion. You can 'view the thread' and thereby see not only the original message but each reply made to it.

Title page
See **index page**.

Upload

To send data from a local computer (ie your computer) to a remote computer (ie someone else's computer). See the opposite, **download**.

URL

Uniform resource location – the unique address of a particular file on the internet. It consists of

protocol   http//:
computer name www.internetforschools.co.uk
path to file   /index.htm

So the full URL would be:
http//:www.internetforschools.co.uk/index.htm

Usenet
This is the general name given to the system of newsgroups available through the internet or bulletin boards. There are well over 30,000 in existence, and the number is growing all the time.

Virtual reality
An artificial environment created with computer hardware and software and presented to the user in such a way that it appears and feels like a real place. The term is currently used to generally refer to any virtual world represented within a computer, even if it is just a text-based or graphical representation. There are many web-based virtual-reality environments for users to explore via the browser.

VRML
Pronounced *vermal*, and short for virtual reality modelling Language, VRML is a specification for displaying 3-dimensional objects on the world wide web. Files written in VRML have a .wrl extension (short for world). To view these, you need a VRML browser or a VRML **plug-in** for your **browser**.

Walled garden
This term is used to describe a filtered internet feed offered to schools by companies such as BT and RM. Other value-added services are often offered such as projects and competitions. These are only available to subscribers.

Web
Shorthand term for the world wide web (WWW).

Web mail
Web mail, or web-based mail, is email that requires a live internet connection for it to be managed, read and sent.

Web site
A world wide web site is made up of many web pages linked together using **hyperlinks**.

Web66
A premier US educational web site. *See* Appendix.

Web-whack
The copying of world wide web pages onto your hard drive so that they can be used as part of an intranet. Name derived from popular software package with similar name.

Welcome page
See index page.

Wild card
A character used in search programs. You can use it to widen your search. For instance a search with the string 'bee*' would find references to Beethoven, beetroot, bees and beer!

Index

Index